100+ Wedding Games

Fun & Laughs for Bachelorette Parties, Showers & Receptions

by Joan Wai

author of
100+ Baby Shower Games

DISCLAIMER

A wedding is a very sensitive time, especially for the marrying couple. Use your common sense and carefully evaluate the appropriateness of these games and pranks to the occasion. Though effort has been made to present these activities as fun for players and spectators, fun and funny can be surprisingly subjective. The publisher and author disclaim any liability, physical or emotional, that may result from proper or improper use of the information herein.

ISBN: 0-9728354-2-3
      978-0-9728354-2-8

Published in the U.S.A. by The Brainstorm Company, 11684 Ventura Blvd. #970, Studio City, CA 91604. www.TheBrainstormCompany.com

Cover and interior illustrations by Jun Falkenstein

CONTENTS

INTRODUCTION

Most people have heard of bachelorette and bridal shower games, many are described in this book. But, "wedding games" are not as rare as you may think. Ever clinked your glass to get newlyweds to kiss? Or dived after the bouquet? Then you already have played a wedding game. In these pages, you will find there are many more fun and unique games to play at a reception.

Wedding games are a popular tradition around the world as ice breakers and personalized entertainment. German, Russian, Mexican, Indian, and Chinese receptions typically serve up wedding games and pranks in between courses.

I'll never forget the first wedding I attended because that's where I witnessed my first wedding game. The reception was for an uncle, I think I was 10. What I recall most clearly was the spontaneous eruption of utensils clinking against glass during the reception dinner. Over 100 friends and family built the tinkling to a glass-shattering roar. When the blushing couple finally rose to their feet to comply with a kiss, the clinking was replaced by applause and feasting resumed. Woe to my ears when the newlyweds pecked lips too chastely for the crowd's taste.

Out of the countless weddings since, the most memorable for me are those where friends organized contests featuring the Bride and Groom. Guests were often invited to participate too. A really great game has the wedding entourage and their guests laughing so hard they're in tears. Now that's a party!

The belief that a jolly atmosphere is integral to a festive wedding drives friends to also visit--or commandeer--the newlywed suite to play tricks and games with the Bride and Groom on their wedding night. The French call this tradition the *charivari*. Germans have a similar ritual, *polterabend*, where friends create a racket by breaking old plates to leave a huge mess on the couple's front doorstep. An old American custom, the shivaree, involves obnoxious music in a mock serenade. Around the world, practical jokes and games are an engaging and charming custom to celebrate the newly wed couple.

Then

As I mentioned, there's one wedding game nearly everybody has played at least once in their life. The bouquet or garter toss.

The toss is said to arise from the medieval practice of friends accompanying the Bride and Groom to their wedding bed. It was considered good luck to tear off a section of the bride's dress, especially since she wasn't going to wear it again. Inebriated crowds allegedly got so unruly that Brides tossed out a garter (and eventually the bouquet) to save her dress and her modesty.

Superstition once held that evil spirits could be warded off the newlyweds by having friends play pranks that pick on the couple. These spirits were expected to take pity and spare the couple any ill fortune. The traditions of the decorated wedding car and honking of car horns (to scare away the bad) resulted.

And Now

Games transform a potentially drawn out meal or gathering into a roll-up your sleeves celebration. Organized activities encourage spirited interaction. They give a chance for the Bride's and Groom's families to bond. And it's an alternative for those guests who can't, don't, or won't dance.

Games also set up great video and picture opportunities. And you never know what new friendships will form and lead to a walk down the aisle among your single guests.

A wedding and its related functions can be a once in a lifetime event. What better excuse do you need to celebrate and have fun?

Let the Games Begin

The many duties that a best man and/or maid of honor may take on include laying down plans to guarantee a blushing Bride (or Groom for that matter). Wedding attendants may lend support as game hosts/referees and/or competitors to set the example for good sportsmanship. Using a microphone is suggested for larger crowds, especially when explaining the game rules to players and observers.

Depending upon the tone of the event and your participants, games are not solely for the reception, shower, or bachelorette party. A formal reception, for instance, may relegate informal antics to other occasions, such as the engagement party, rehearsal dinner, bridal luncheon, or the morning after brunch. Once the festivities are over, hang onto this book for an anniversary party, or adapt the games to family reunions.

The games in this book are categorized by the way they're played:

- ❑ **Speed Games**
  challenge a player's agility, speed, and/or coordination
- ❑ **Sit Down Games**
  can be played sitting down
- ❑ **Memory/Word Games**
  utilize memorization and/or word play

- ❏ **Active Games**
  require some freedom of movement, but speed is
  not necessarily an advantage
- ❏ **Fun Activities**
  are not games in the strictest sense, but still
  entertaining to do
- ❏ **Pranks**
  a little comedy at the Bride or Groom's expense

Allow about 15 minutes or less to play each game. See the Game
& Activity Index for additional suggestions on what games are likely to
appeal to various occasions.

Keep It Sweet

Sense of humor is highly subjective. A good host is sensitive to the
sensibilities of the Bride and Groom and their guests. Discuss your
intentions with the couple ahead of time. If they're very private or shy
people, honor their request to avoid revealing too much personal
information or overly embarrassing them in front of extended friends
and family. And if you do plan a prank and you're single, remember
that makes you fair game when your wedding comes around.

Games with a risqué theme are best reserved for a bachelorette
party. Unattached people tend to be more receptive than established
couples to games that require trading intimate knowledge or touching
other guests. If you're still not sure what games are right for your
crowd, consider sampling one game from each chapter. It should
quickly become obvious by player enthusiasm and energy level what
the group favors.

Awarding prizes are not necessary, but do give guests extra
incentive to put their all into a competition. Threatening losers with
performing a penalty is another option to elicit more effort from jaded
players.

A Wedding to Remember

While being a good host generally means involving everyone, total
group participation cannot be expected or forced. Many of these
competitions are as enjoyable to spectators as the good sports who
join in. These games are intended to be light-hearted and upbeat in
tone, setup and play them with that in mind. Your guests will leave the
wedding with happy memories and new friends!

SPEED GAMES

ARMFUL OF BABIES

Get busy diapering as many flour children as you can.

When
Coed/all girls bachelorette/shower

How
This is a race to see who can diaper the most babies. Players assume the role of caretaker one at a time at a table. Have ready on the table 10 – 5 lb. bags of flour (your babies), a roll of paper towels (your diapers) and adhesive tape (to impersonate safety pins).

Using one sheet of paper towel as a diaper, the caretaker must quickly wrap the diaper around the bottom of the bag and affix with tape. The caretaker then must hold the diapered babe (cradle in arm, hand, between the legs--be creative) while diapering the next infant. The task gets more difficult as more babies get diapered. A player's turn ends whenever they accidentally drop a bundle of joy.

Remove any diapers on the babies before starting the next player's turn. After everybody has gone a round, award prizes to the diaper king and queen who successfully wrapped the most babies.

Variation/Tips
❑ Use disposable diapers or cloth diapers and safety pins (no poking into the baby!) instead of paper towels and tape.

❑ Seal each bag of flour in plastic wrap to prevent leaks. Reinforce the babies for multiple diaperings with a strip of duct tape around the middle of your kiddies (their "waist").

❑ Embellish each bag of flour with kiddie items: a different colored bonnet, pacifier, or bib etc. for comic effect.

❑ Light a fire under competitors by putting a time limit of 5 minutes or less to diaper as many wee ones as they can.

BEAUTY SCHOOL

The quickest study of the closest shave wins.

When
Coed shower/bachelorette/reception

How
Have ready: a can of shaving cream, 3 spoons, 6 large plastic trash bags. Cut a slit in the bottom seam of each bag about the length of your hand. Players will use this bag as a bib to protect their clothing by sticking their head through the hole in the upside down bag.

To start beauty school, arrange three chairs about three feet apart before your audience. Select three guys (preferably clean shaven) and three gals to play. Sit each guy in a chair and stand a woman next to each guy. Let the men don their shaving bibs (offer the women a bib, if they use one you'll need to slit the sides of the bags for their arms). Give each woman a spoon. Quickly spray the same amount of shaving cream on all of the men's cheeks and chin.

The beauticians have 30 seconds to use their spoon to "shave" all the cream off their client's face. The gal who gives her man the closest shave (removes the most cream) wins!

Variations/Tips
❑   Offer the Bride and Groom the option to participate as a team. Give each a trash bag bib to protect their clothing.
❑   Lay newspaper under each chair for easy clean-up afterward.
❑   Have just the men compete in blindfolds. Arm your blind barbers with a spoon, then spray shaving cream on their faces. They have 45 seconds to "shave" themselves as cleanly as possible.
❑   If the women are game, sit them in the barber's chair and pull their pant leg or skirt up to their knee to reveal one leg. Apply shaving cream to the length of the leg and blindfold the men, see how quickly they can clean off their partner's leg with a spoon.

BIG BALLS

Teams get ballsy with a lemon dangling between their legs.

When
Coed/all girls bachelorette/shower

How
Have two pairs of old pantyhose (keep extra pairs on hand in case your hosiery gets a massive run) and four lemons ready. Drop one lemon into just one leg of each pair, set aside the extra two lemons.

Divide the group in half (or have boys versus girls). One member from each team ties the pantyhose around their waist so that the socked lemon dangles between their legs at knee level. Place the other lemon in front of each team. The object is to keep swinging their pantyhose lemon until they knock the free lemon across a designated line in the room. Mark a start and finish line (about 12 feet apart) in the room or simply designate that the lemon must touch opposite walls on the playing field.

Once a ball boy or girl finishes whacking their lemon across the room, they give their pantyhose to the next player on their team who now has to knock the loose lemon to the opposite line. Keep the ball rolling until all the members of one team have had a complete turn. The team that finishes first can say they got the defeated team by the balls.

Variation/Tips
❑ Try substituting lemons with oranges, softballs, or even balloons.
❑ In lieu of rolling an object across the room, simplify the game by setting an unopened soda can in front of each player. Whoever knocks over the can in front of them first wins.

BLOW A KISS

Teamwork and loose lips will win this kiss off.

When
Coed bachelorette/shower/reception

How
You'll need 10 drinking straws, 2 business cards, and 10 players (it could be 5 bridesmaids and 5 groomsmen for example). Divide the players into 2 teams, each team forms a line. Give each player a straw. Each line races to relay the card from first player to the last player in line the fastest, using only their straw.

The head of each team starts with a business card, the "kiss." A player inhales through the straw to suction the card onto their end of the straw. While sucking on the card, they pass the card to the next player in their line. The receiving player uses their straw to suck on the card (the passing player should stop sucking, or blow, to release). The next player passes it to the next and so on.

Fastest team to complete the kiss blowing relay wins. If a player drops the card, they may pick it up with their hand to reattach it to their straw and resume blowing the kiss down the line.

Variation/Tips
- ❑ To make it easier to hold the card, shorten the straws by cutting them in half before the race. The team leader may use their hand to hold the card to their straw, but once the race is on, they must let go of the card and rely on suction only.
- ❑ Expand game to include more players, just get more straws.
- ❑ For a more intimate game, ditch the straws.
- ❑ If the game blows, try this version. Have players race to pass a drinking straw (or chopstick) down the line by holding the straw horizontally between their upper lip and nose (in other words, they have to pucker to hold and transfer the straw).
- ❑ There are many variations of this relay race. A popular one is to pass an orange by cradling it between your shoulder and cheek only. Or, pass a long balloon between the knees or under the arm pit.

COOKING UP DINNER

Never thought the ruse to substitute take-out for a homemade meal could be turned into a game, did ya?

When
All girls bachelorette/shower

How
Put a prize in a medium-sized box. Tightly and securely wrap the box with 15 layers of gift wrap and some occasional curling ribbon. You'll also need a pair of dice and clothing befitting of a chef: an apron, two pairs of oven mitts, and a chef's hat.

Players sit on the floor and form a circle. Tell the group that they burnt dinner and guests are expected. Now they have to serve take-out as home cooked before their unsuspecting honey and guests arrive. To start, give a player (your chef) the wrapped present (the "to-go box") and the apron, oven mitts, and chef's hat. Give a pair of dice to the player sitting left of your chef. At the word "go," the player with the dice continuously rolls the dice until she gets doubles. At the same time, the chef must quickly don the chef's get-up, then try to unwrap the box one layer at a time--all before the dice player rolls doubles.

When doubles are rolled, everything gets passed left to the next player. Now it's the former dice player's turn to rush into the cook's outfit and try to open the to-go box while the new dice holder rolls for doubles. Whoever successfully opens the box keeps the prize inside.

Variation/Tips
❑ An actual chef's toque can be pricey. Unless you already have one, adequate substitutions include a paper hat or baseball cap (worn backwards of course!) or hair net.

EAT THE PICKLE

Competition to tickle the pickle.

When
Coed/all girls bachelorette

How
Buy a large jar of whole pickles, the bigger the better. Tie a clothesline across the room. Use string to tie the pickle to the clothesline, adjusting the height for each person who's game. The pickle should hang in front of each person's mouth.

To play, contestants must keep their hands behind their backs. At a given signal, participants have 30 seconds to see who can munch the most green. Winner is the one who has eaten the most of their pickle.

Variation/Tips
❑ Lay newspaper underneath the contestants to make clean-up easier. Provide bibs to protect your guest's clothing.
❑ If enough players dislike pickles, substitute similar sized carrots or cucumbers.
❑ Use a small unpeeled banana in lieu of a pickle. Players have to figure out a way to peel the banana with their teeth, then eat it. Scrub the bananas clean beforehand! And make sure they're of similar length for fair play.
❑ A way more risqué variation: while seated, each player holds a banana upright between their knees. With their eyes closed, they race to be first to open a (non-lubricated) condom and unroll it completely onto their banana.

FEEL EACH OTHER OUT

Bride gives her sweetheart the once over with Russian fingers and Roman hands.

When
Coed bachelorette/reception

How
Attach three small binder clips (or paperclips) wherever you dare on the Groom's clothing. Blindfold the Bride and tell her she has one minute to find all three clips.

Variation/Tips
❑ The smaller the clips, the harder they will be to find. To really stump the Bride, put a clip on the Groom's shoelaces.

❑ Make the Bride perform a penalty for each clip she fails to find.

❑ Or, Groom performs a penalty for each clip the Bride finds.

❑ Reverse roles so that the Groom searches his Bride for clips.

❑ Substitute gummy candies and tie them to the Bride's dress with a bit of ribbon. The Groom has to locate the candies with his mouth only. Extend the time limit to two minutes.

❑ This game is easily expanded to include other players in a Jack and Jill party. Simply pair up boy/girl combinations and let teams compete to be the first to find all the clips.

Carefully maneuver a sausage into its target.

When
Coed/all girl's bachelorette/shower

How
Prepare one hot dog per player like this: Poke a hole on the side of the wiener about one inch from an end and tie with a piece of twine (about 12 inches in length) to that end. Take the other end of the twine and tie it onto a player's back belt loop. (Use more twine to loop around the waist if players don't have belt loops to tie the dog onto.) The hot dog should dangle freely behind your player's behind.

Set an empty milk bottle in front of each player. At the word "Go!" players squat to get their wiener completely into the bottle. First one to succeed shouts, "I'm in!" and receives top dog honors.

Variations/Tips
❑ Use Bratwursts instead of puny hot dogs. The mere sight of these props will evoke giggles. Of course, you'll need to find something with a wider opening, such as a jelly or pasta sauce jar.

❑ Try cocktail sausages instead of hot dogs. Use jars with smaller openings, such as baby food jars.

❑ If sausage meat is too uncomfortable, figuratively and literally, for the players, substitute a zucchini or baby carrot instead.

❑ The more narrow you make the bottle opening, the more challenging the game becomes.

❑ If you don't have milk bottles, try small-mouthed jars or milk jugs filled with some sand so they don't tip over too easily.

❑ Scatter a handful of tacks in the bottom of the jar and set a one-minute time-limit. Competitors have to dip their dog into the jar and maneuver the sausage to pick up as many tacks as they can. The one who picks up the most tacks is the winner.

INVESTMENT SCHEME

Bank on this ticklish money laundering race for lots of laughs.

When
Coed bachelorette/reception

How
Call up three guys and three gals. Pair each guy with a gal so that there are three two-person teams. Each man represents a business and each woman is a venture capitalist with money to invest.

Give each capitalist 30 bills in play money. She has one minute to fully fund her company by tucking the bills wherever she dares in her male partner's clothing. Advise the dollar dames to spread the green stuff around and invest securely by hiding the cash the best they can.

Once time is up, inform the financiers that their business is being reorganized. Have the men switch investors (go to a different female partner). The investor's job now is to try to recoup all the assets she can from the investment scheme--that is, find and collect all the money hidden in their new partner. The collector who can flash the most cash after thirty seconds is your breadwinner!

Variation/Tips
- ❑ To expand the men's role in the game, ask them to specify what business they will embody to entice investors. Suggest a fantasy start-up, such as a Donut Factory or the John Doe Foundation for the Arts. Announce their picks to the gathering before starting the financing feud.
- ❑ If established couples want to play this game, begin the investment round with mismatched couples, then reunite couples for the withdrawal round. Or, spice it up by letting couples invest, then change partners for the pull-out.
- ❑ The men are not allowed to reveal where the money's hidden nor can they help by removing the money themselves.
- ❑ To make the game more innocent for a reception, tell players they may only put money outside their partner's clothing (in other words, no skin contact--they may tuck bills into sleeves, collars, pockets, belts, etc.).
- ❑ Or, have the men hide the money on themselves first without telling them why, then unleash the women on them.
- ❑ Declare that torn money does not count toward the total.

LICK THE DONUT

A game to get everybody licking their lips.

When
Coed/all girls bachelorette

How
Purchase enough mini donuts powdered in white sugar so that there's at least one for each player. Prep the game by hanging a clothesline across the room where you'll be playing. Use a piece of string to tie the donut to the clothesline so that it dangles in front of a player's mouth.

Pick three players to compete at a time. At the word "Go," first person to lick the donut clean without breaking the donut or biting it wins. Recruit another group of three for the next competition. Then, have a run off between the winners from the two rounds.

Variation/Tips
❑ Provide a time limit of 60 seconds to see who has the fastest working tongue.
❑ Ask everybody to participate in the race at once and see who gets it licked.
❑ Make players spin three complete circles before getting in their licks.

LOSE THE DIME

She's getting hitched, her dime be ditched.

When
Coed/all girls bachelorette/shower

How
There's an old saying that if you don't want to get pregnant, you'd better put a dime in between your knees. Now that the lovely Bride is acquiring a husband, it's safe to drop the dime--literally.

You'll need five clean baby food jars (or baby bottles) and five dimes so that five players can play at a time. (If you have more than five players who want to play, start another round with a new group after finishing the first contest.)

Assemble the jars three feet apart in one row. Have the players start ten feet away from the jars and give each a dime to hold in between their knees. At the word "Go!" players must waddle their dime over to the jar and drop the coin into their jar. First to complete this task wins. Players who drop their dime before they reach the jar or miss the jar must return and do it over from the starting point.

If multiple winners are a dime a dozen (perhaps you've got three winners from three competitions of five players), have a run-off and increase the distance between the starting point and the jar.

Variation/Tips
❏   Give players quarters if they're having too much difficulty with a dime.

MUSHY LOVE

The Groom gets mushy with his honey bun.

When
Coed bachelorette/shower/reception

How
Announce that this is a test of the Bride and Groom's abilities to provide for and feed one another. Position the two so that they're standing face to face, hands behind their backs. Give the Groom an individual serving of a snack cake still in its wrapper to hold in his mouth. The couple must work together to open the package and eat the entire cake without the use of their hands. Give them 45 seconds to get sweet with one another. If they drop the treat before they finish it, they have to get mushy all over again.

It's all sweetness and light when they win. But if they fail, sugarcoat the news that they get another chance with an extended time limit of 60 seconds. Most couples should succeed within one minute as this "test" is rigged to produce winners.

Variation/Tips
❑   Provide a bib to both players for easier clean-up afterwards.
❑   Include couples among the competitors. Award a prize to whichever team finishes first.

OPEN HOUSE

A home drawing competition to bring down the house.

When
Coed/all girls shower/reception

How
Call up seven people to play, these are your architects. Give each designer a large paper plate and a felt pen (or crayon). Instruct them to flip the plate over and print their name on the bottom of the plate.

Thank your artists for volunteering to draw a dream house for the Bride and Groom. They put the plate (right side up) on top of their head and use their pen to draw a home sweet home on the inside of the plate. At the word "Go!" they have 30 seconds to drive home their masterpiece.

When time's up, collect the plates and send the architects homeward to their seats. Show the houses to the newlywed couple, try to get a comment from them for each plate of real estate. Once they've homed in on their favorite house, flip the plate over to announce the designer who scored the home run.

Variation/Tips

❑ Use a microphone to broadcast the Bride and Groom's reactions to the neighborhood of freshly built homes. A fast-thinking emcee may want to gently tease the architects for some laughs.

❑ Instead of calling up volunteers at the reception, have each table send a member to this house party.

❑ Let guests vote. Tape plates in a row to a wall and a blank sheet of paper below each homemade house. Provide a pen for guests to make one mark under their favorite during the reception. Declare the winner before the end of the party.

❑ In lieu of drawing homes, try the wedding bouquet, dress, or cake.

❑ Instead of drawing on their head, have the artists do their homework while sitting at a table with the plate in front of them-- but they cannot lift their pen while drawing.

❑ If paper plates aren't readily available, use regular paper and a magazine or book as a drawing surface.

PINCHING PENNIES

Try making a run for the money through a cluttered purse.

When
All girls bachelorette/shower

How
Fill a very large bowl (a punch bowl is great) with uncooked white rice grains (at least 2 pounds). Mix in 25 pennies. This bowl of rice will serve as the mother of all disorganized purses.

Challenge players one at a time to find as many coins as they can within one minute--while blindfolded. Replenish the rice with money after each play. The one who pinches out the most pennies cashes in for a reward.

Variation/Tips
- ❑ Don't blindfold players and give them only 30 seconds to grab as many coins as they can.
- ❑ Add one additional rule, for each grain of rice they spill, an equal number of coins are taken away from their "found" pile.
- ❑ Mix 10 paperclips into the rice to serve as red herrings.
- ❑ Discard the rice after play.

POP THE QUESTION

Bang out trivia questions about the lucky couple.

When
Coed shower/bachelorette/reception

How
Write a simple trivia question about the Bride or Groom on an index card sized piece of paper. Insert the paper in a large balloon and partially blow it up, then tie it off. Prepare four more large balloons the same way, inserting a different trivia question in each.

Select five couples to play. Give each couple a balloon, they must stand face to face while holding the balloon between their stomachs, their hands stay behind their backs.

At the word "Go," couples race to be the first to pop their balloon by squeezing the balloon between them. First to couple to go out with a bang and answer their trivia question correctly wins.

Variation/Tips
❑ See Appendix for sample trivia questions. Neatly print the questions so they're easy to read.

❑ The less inflated the balloon, the less taut it is, and the harder it'll be to pop. Try to blow the balloons about 1/4 to 1/5 short of its normal size.

❑ To keep playing after the first couple succeeds, see if the next couple to pop their balloon can answer their trivia question correctly, continue until every balloon gets popped.

❑ If desired, use ribbon to tie the balloon to one player's waist (on each team) to help keep the balloon in place.

❑ A less physical variation: couples stand face to face, holding their palms out, touching their partners only at the palms. Then with their eyes closed, every player spins in place five complete turns. The first couple to match up with their partner's palms gets a trivia question. If they answer correctly, they win.

POPPING THE CHERRY

The cherry-lipped Bride and Groom go head to head.

When
Reception

How
Get a cherry that still has its stem attached. Tie a piece of string to the stem. Stand up on a chair so that you can dangle the cherry just above the newlyweds' mouths. Their job is nibble to the pit as quickly as they can. Whoever nabs the pit between their teeth first wins. You can make the game harder by not holding the cherry still.

Variation/Tips
❑ In case of a significant height difference between the Bride and Groom, sit them down in chairs facing each other. To further equalize your players, use a telephone book or two as a booster seat.

❑ A similar contest is to place a single cherry in two glass bowls, one goes in front of the Bride and one before the Groom. Tell them the object is to be the first to eat their cherry without using their hands. When the couple declare they're ready to start, fill the bowls with whipped cream and then shout "Go!"

❑ Cherries out of season? Substitute a small apricot or plum, tie with a piece of kitchen twine.

❑ This variation has the Groom simply hold the fruit (a fresh or dried cherry, strawberry, or fig will do) between his teeth, challenging the Bride to get her half (and stealing a public kiss in the process). Of course, he shouldn't make it easy by twisting away and the Bride has to figure out how to outwit the Groom. Invite a few other couples to demonstrate how to play this game before the Bride and Groom. This is a chance for hams in the audience to shine.

THE SHORTEST CARROT

Guests try to pass a shrinking carrot between their legs.

When
Coed/all girls bachelorette/shower

How
Start with one long carrot. Have guests stand two feet from one another. The first player takes the carrot between their knees and passes it onto the next player, who also takes it with their knees and passes it on. Keep transferring the vegetable until someone drops it.

Each time someone drops the carrot, cut an inch off the carrot. The last player to successfully take the stubby veggie without dropping it wins.

Variation/Tips
❑ Any elongated vegetable, such as an English cucumber or Chinese radish, makes an entertaining substitute.

❑ If your players are particularly skilled at carrying the carrot and nobody lets it drop after many passes, add the rule that after every fifth pass, a cut will be made.

❑ Twist the game a bit by having guests stand in a circle while passing a large and long balloon between their knees around the group. They keep passing while music plays. Whoever's caught holding the balloon whenever the music stops must withdraw from the group. Last one standing wins.

SOMETHING OLD, NEW, BORROWED, AND BLUE

A quick scavenger hunt for unique items that fulfill the traditional Bride's mantra.

When
Coed/all girls bachelorette

How
Have teams of players race to bring back the most items from a list. Create a list inspired by the Victorian era rhyme that's supposed to bring good-luck to the Bride who heeds this advice when assembling her gown: "Something old, something new, something borrowed, something blue."

Create four columns on the list. Something old: newspaper from last week, shoe from the side of the road, movie stub. Something new: an unopened condom, fresh flower, crisp $20 bill. Something borrowed: a rented video, card from a car rental agency, picture of a wedding. Something blue: a blue tissue, blue key chain, blue music CD.

Divide players into two or more teams. Pass out the lists and give them one hour to return. Give one point for each item they bring back. Declare an extra point will be awarded for each item that is creative or unusual. The host and/or Bride make judgement calls when needed and declare the victorious team.

Variation/Tips
❑ Bring players to a mall and modify the scavenger list to things that can be found within mall stores.
❑ Rather keep the party together? Modify the list so that it's doable within the vicinity of the hosting home.
❑ A more cooperative game is to have all work together at seeking out items on the list during a night of bar-hopping. In which case, the list could be modified to require players to obtain items from total strangers (for example: a blue watch, a new roll of breath mints, a borrowed wallet, an old leather jacket, etc.).

SPOONING

Practice the fine art of cleaning house.

When
Coed/all girls bachelorette/shower

How
A player has to kneel or sit on the floor to play. Place a large plastic bowl before her and sprinkle about 40 cotton balls on the floor around the bowl. Give the player a pair of oven mitts to put over her hands, then hand her a wooden stirring spoon. Using the spoon only, she must scoop and place as many dust bunnies (the cotton balls) as she can into the bowl within 30 seconds.

Keep track of how many balls each player gets into the bowl. The one who got the most cotton balls in leaves the losers in the dust.

Variation/Tips
❑   Blindfold players and see how many cotton balls they can pick up using their oven mitts. To really make the dust fly, require blindfolded competitors to use the spoon.
❑   To make this dust off easier, pour 40 cotton balls in another bowl and set the cotton bowl about a foot away from the empty bowl. Challenge blindfolded players to transfer the balls between bowls with the spoon.
❑   This game can be easily adapted for play while seated at a table. Lay a fabric tablecloth on the table (provides more traction). Seat a player in front of a table with the props to play. Any balls that fall off the table can not be returned to the table, so the player needs to be extra careful when moving the balls.
❑   If 30 seconds isn't enough time, extend the time limit.

STICK IT

Erotically charged race to thread a roll of toilet paper.

When
Coed/all girls bachelorette

How
Divide the group into pairs. Have two pairs compete at a time to see which team can run a broom handle through a roll of toilet paper the fastest. Sounds easy right? Explain that one person holds the broom between their legs, while the other holds the toilet paper roll between their legs, and they have to work together to guide the broom handle through the roll.

Each pair gets one broom and a roll of toilet paper. The broom holder holds the broom between their upper thighs with the broom handle pointing out (bristle end is behind them). The other person on the team holds the roll between their thighs (hole facing out). The pair (consisting of one broom holder and one roll holder) face each other and hold hands. Blindfold the broomstick holder on each team. Tell the players to start.

The sighted player can guide their partner with verbal instructions. They can not let go of each other's hands. Once a roll is on the stick, the roll holder announces their success. The pair that finishes this task first can brag that they have the thunder down under.

Variation/Tips
❑   Increase the difficulty by making each team thread an additional two rolls of toilet paper onto the same stick, but one roll at a time. The holder must carefully squeeze all three rolls between their legs for their partner to thread.
❑   Make this a relay. Divide pairs into two teams and when one pair succeeds in "sticking it," they must pass on their props to the next pair. First team to finish wins.
❑   Substitute a chopstick and empty soda bottle between their legs. The pair have to place the chopstick in the open bottle.

TIE THE KNOT

The Bride and Groom show off their love knot.

When
Coed bachelorette/shower/reception

How
Tell the Bride and Groom that they have another chance to tie the knot (if it's a reception) or to rehearse tying the knot (if it's before the wedding). Give them a one foot long section of thick rope (1/8" to 1/4" in diameter, usually available at hardware stores).

Give the couple one minute to tie the rope into a big and tight knot to demonstrate their close knit love for one another. However, they must do so with one hand behind their backs!

Most couples will succeed in creating a knot of some sort within one minute as this "challenge" always produces a winner.

Variation/Tips
❑ Select a child to see if s/he can undo the knot within a minute.

❑ A more challenging variation: select a child to tie the rope into a complicated knot before the game. The Bride and Groom must work together to unravel their knotty problem, while holding one hand behind their backs, to display their teamwork. Allow the couple up to five minutes to undo the tied up rope.

❑ Even tougher: the maid of honor or Groom's sister ties a knot that the couple have to unravel together (using both hands). The more quickly the couple can untangle the knot, according to Indian tradition, the more quickly success will come to them.

❑ Adapt the game to include other couples: select five couples to play. Offer five pieces of rope to different members of the wedding party to tie into different knots. Randomly give a knot to each couple. Each player holds a hand behind their back while working as a couple to be the first to undo their knot.

❑ Or, tie a couple knots around the Bride and Groom's wrist. They take turns trying to undo the knot on their partner's wrist.

TOILET PAPER GOWNS

Become the Bride's personal designer of toilet paper couture.

When
Coed/all girls bachelorette/shower

How
Create teams of up to four members each. You want at least two competing teams. Give each team three rolls of toilet paper and one roll of clear tape (you can opt to not offer tape, but more elaborate gowns can be made with tape). Each team selects one person to be their model.

All teams have 15 minutes to create a wedding gown for their selected model. At the end of the competition, the models show off their team's creations and the Bride announces her favorite, funniest, or most fanciful, etc.

Variation/Tips

❑ Toilet Paper or Tissue Veil. Instead of a gown, each team puts their creative efforts into making a veil for the Bride within a 10 minute time period. You can provide unlimited amounts of paper, or in the case of tissues, put on a limit of 3 sheets per person. That's not much, but necessity is the mother of invention.

❑ Open the creative floodgates by letting each person create anything they think the Bride will need for her wedding day: a ring pillow, lingerie, etc. with their limited/unlimited allotment of paper. Or, have the women fashion tuxedos for the men.

❑ The Ultimate Feminine Veil. In addition to toilet/tissue paper, give each team a handful of feminine napkins and tampons to use as decorative flourishes.

❑ If a veil is particularly well done, the Bride may elect to wear it for the rest of the party or during rehearsal.

❑ Tissue Paper Gown. Guests are given one sheet of tissue paper (the thin stuff that's used to cushion gifts) and they all must work together to dress the Bride in a gown. Also provide three rolls of clear tape. Give them 20 minutes to complete their task.

❑ Have teams model their creations for the group to music.

❑ To get creative juices flowing quickly, suggest fashioning a garter, veil, purse, train, bodice, skirt, shoes, etc.

❑ After gowns are completed, give every guest a paper plate and a pen. Tell them they have 3 minutes to sketch the winning gown on the plate--but the plate has to be placed on the top of the drawer's head while sketching the gown. Let the Bride judge the winning rendition.

❏ Turn the game on its head by having your designers fashion bridesmaid or mother-in-law gowns instead of wedding dresses.

❏ If the group is small, have everyone work together to create one single dress for the Bride out of toilet paper.

❏ Double the time allotment for more elaborate results.

WAKE-UP CALL
Find a ringing alarm clock before time runs out.

When
Coed/all girls bachelorette

How
One person in the group is sent out of the room. The rest of the group set an alarm clock to go off in three minutes and decide where to hide the alarm clock. Call the player back in the room when the clock starts to ring. If the player succeeds in finding the clock before it stops ringing, they escape a penalty. If the player fails, the group decides a penalty for the player.

Variation/Tips
❏ If requiring shots of liquor as a penalty, spread out play so that this hide and seek drinking game is played once every half-hour. This helps prevent players from getting too drunk.

❏ Give the game a randy turn by substituting a new vibrator for the ringing clock. Use a stopwatch to give the player a half a minute to seek out the good vibrations.

❏ For a quieter game, have everybody close their eyes. Select one person to put a penny somewhere in the room. It must be in plain sight, just not immediately obvious (at the base of a TV, for example; it cannot be inside a drawer or under books). All players then open their eyes and search for the penny. The goal is not to be the last one to find it. Players who spot the coin leave the penny where it is, but must confirm the sighting with the person who positioned it.

SIT DOWN GAMES

ALL ABOUT ME

Armchair detectives must deduce just the lies, ma'am.

When
Coed/all girl's bachelorette/shower

How
Instruct players to introduce him/herself by telling the group three things about themselves, two must be true and one must be a lie. The remainder of the group decide by consensus which statement is not true. The player then reveals the fib.

The game continues with the next person until everybody's had a turn. This game can have multiple winners, those who succeed in pulling the wool over their audience's eyes earn bragging rights.

Variation/Tips
❑ Advise tongue-tied guests to theme the three statements together. It can be about their cooking, driving, gardening, work, or bedroom abilities--whatever they feel comfortable revealing and will make for compelling conversation. For example, a guest might declare: "I've totaled my car once. I failed my driver's test twice. And I got ticketed for driving the wrong way on a street once."

❑ The host should go first, giving everybody time to spin up creative yarns.

❑ To encourage more clever deception, award a prize to players who are able to hoodwink the others.

❑ This variation simplifies the game. Have each player flip a coin before they speak. If it comes up heads, they tell one true fact about themselves, if it comes up tails, they tell a lie. Guests (who do not see the result of the coin toss) have to guess if the information was truth or a lie.

BEST GUESS
A marital aid mystery.

When
Coed/all girls bachelorette/shower

How
Purchase 5 unusual items from an adult toy store. Ideally, they should lack an obvious purpose when removed from their packaging. Give every participant a pad and pen. Hold up each item for about 30 seconds at a time. Ask players to write what they think the object is and what it's supposed to do.

At the end of the game, everyone reads their answer for each object, you then reveal each object's true purpose. A point is given per correct answer. Player who scores big wins a toy.

Variation/Tips
❑ Keep the game fast paced to maintain interest. Allow about 30 seconds for guests to write their answer, remind them to be brief, then introduce the next item.

❑ For a less risqué version, use exotic kitchen gadgets, such as a wooden juice reamer, zester, bowl scraper etc. to test your guests' cooking savvy.

❑ Among the pack of marital aids, throw in a specialized kitchen gadget; or if using kitchen gadgets, throw in a marital aid for laughs.

❑ For more challenging game play, put each gadget in a sock or paper bag and let people make their guess based on what they can feel through the bag.

BOOZE HOUND

Identify 10 shots by what the nose knows.

When
Coed/all girls bachelorette/shower

How
Prepare 10 shot glasses of different flavored liquors. Number each glass. Let players smell each shot glass in turn and write down their guess for each glass. When all 10 shot glasses have made their rounds, announce the correct answers and see who has the sharpest nasal ability.

Variations/Tips

❑ If this is a drinking crowd that "needs" a little extra help, let everyone take a sip of each before guessing.

❑ To make the game more challenging, fill shot glasses with the same kind of liquor, but vary the brand names.

❑ For a non-alcoholic variation of this game, use a variety of juices: tomato, orange, strawberry, guava, peach, etc., and test the sharpness of everyone's noses or taste buds.

The unwrapping of gifts becomes a bingo pull for attendees.

When
Coed/all girls shower

How
To prepare for this game, ask the Bride not to open any presents she receives before the shower. You'll need at least 15 unopened gifts to play. Create a blank BINGO card (sample provided in the Appendix) for every person attending the shower. Fill in the squares with gifts that were on the Bride's gift registry. Vary the placement of the gifts from square to square so that no card is exactly alike.

When it's time to open gifts, give everyone a BINGO card and a handful of beans. If the Bride opens a present that's a toaster oven, guests look on their cards for the words "toaster oven" and put a bean on that square in their card. The guest who is first to have beans in either a horizontal or vertical row shouts "Bingo!" A bridesmaid verifies the win and awards the guest a prize.

The Bride continues opening gifts and guests keep racing to declare bingo until all gifts have been opened.

Variation/Tips
❑   A simpler way to play: provide blank bingo cards to each guest and let each participant fill in the squares on their own card with items they predict the Bride will receive before gift opening commences. Then, proceed with normal play.

BUDGET BUSTER

Guess if the price is right for household items.

When
Coed/all girls bachelorette/shower/reception

How
Purchase 5 to 10 household items ahead of time (toilet paper, cleaning supplies, a bag of flour, etc.) and save the receipt.

Recruit three contestants from the group for this home economics quiz. Hold up one item at a time and ask each player to guess the price. Reveal the correct cost of the product and give a small chip (or clothespin, paperclip, play money, etc.) to the one whose stated price was closest without going over.

The winning contestant is the one with the most number of chips in the end.

Variations/Tips
❑ Instead of having players guess the price of each individual item, have them generate a total of all the items. The winner will be closest (in either direction) to the correct total. All attendees can participate in this variation.

❑ Among the household items, include some off-brand items too.

❑ This game can be turned into a reception game by having the Bride and Groom compete against each other. The items should be a mix of career and household items, like a pen or pad of paper, in addition to things like a box of brownie mix, disposable diapers, and so on.

CELEBRITY BRIDES

Challenge guests to identify celebrities in bridal gowns.

When
Coed/all girls bachelorette/shower

How
Clip 10 full-length pictures of bridal gowns out of magazines. Cut out 10 faces of famous women from celebrity magazines and paste each face on top of a bridal gown. Affix these famous brides to white paper and write a number on each sheet of paper.

Pass out the bridal pictures to guests and have them write down the number of the bride and who they think the celebrity is. Announce whoever identifies the most brides correctly will be crowned top celebrity watcher.

Variation/Tips
❑ Add the face of a famous guy for giggles.

❑ Cut out pictures of famous Brides and their Grooms, and write a number next to each woman and letter next to each man. Challenge players to correctly match up the couples by writing their answers on a piece of paper.

CHATTY BLOSSOMS

Learn to speak the language of flowers.

When
Coed/all girls shower

How
Duplicate this quiz for each player:

During the Victorian era, flowers communicated messages to the receiver. The composition of a floral note explains why a full bloom rose (I love you) comes with fern (sincerity) and baby's breath (ever lasting love). Write the letter of the meaning next to each flower.

1) Gardenia
2) pink Carnation
3) Sweet Peas
4) Bells of Ireland
5) Calla Lily
6) Begonia
7) white Chrysanthemum
8) Lily of the Valley
9) Daisy
10) Forget-Me-Not
11) purple Hyacinth
12) Mistletoe

A) good-bye
B) innocence
C) return to happiness
D) memories
E) I'll never forget you
F) secret love
G) kiss me
H) I'm sorry/forgive me
I) truth
J) beauty
K) beware
L) good luck

Variation/Tips

❑ Answers: Gardenia: F; pink Carnation: E; Sweet Peas: A; Bells of Ireland: L; Calla Lily: J; Begonia: K; white Chrysanthemum: I; Lily of the Valley: C; Daisy: B; Forget-Me-Not: D; purple Hyacinth: H; Mistletoe: G

❑ Cut pictures of flowers from the quiz out of wedding magazines and paste them into a reference chart to pass around.

❑ If pencil and paper games wilt your interest, simply turn this into a verbal quiz for players to shout out their answers.

COLD HANDS, WARM HEART

Who can mend fences the fastest by melting an icy heart?

When
Coed/all girls bachelorette/shower

How
You'll need to make ice hearts before the game. Fill an ice cube tray halfway with water and freeze. Once the water freezes, put one red heart-shaped cinnamon candy on each cube and fill tray to the top with water. You want the candy to freeze in the center of the cube. Make enough frozen hearts for each person attending, keep in the freezer until ready to play. Have an equal number of small plastic cups on hand.

Tell a brief story to guests about a fight the Bride and Groom recently had. (This can be a true anecdote if the couple don't mind sharing, or craft an innocuous disagreement like who loves the other more.) Because relations have turned chilly between the couple, the gang is asked to put their hearts into warming theirs.

Give each player a frosty heart in a small cup. Whoever can completely defrost a heart the fastest (that is, melt the entire cube) has patched up the couple's relationship first. What's a better prize than that?

The only rules: players can not remove the cube from the cup or touch the cube in any way. But they can do whatever they wish with the cup as long as the cube stays inside.

Variation/Tips
- If the candy heart floats off to the side of the cube when adding water, use a toothpick to rearrange it before freezing.
- Use this race to occupy guests while the Bride opens her gifts.
- Divide the room in half, one side represents the Bride, the other the Groom. If a heart on the Groom's side thaws out first, make the Groom kiss his Bride wherever designated by the winning heart thawer. Vice versa if the Bride's side wins.

FAMOUS PAIRS

Romantically link together well-known sweethearts.

When
Coed/all girls shower/bachelorette

How
Before the party, prepare a game sheet with two columns. Think of 10 famous couples. These couples might be Ward and June (Cleaver), Elvis & Priscilla (Presley), Gomez & Morticia (Addams). See the Appendix for a sample list. On the left column of your game sheet, write a list of the guy's first names. On the right column, list your female first names, jumbling their order so that no woman's name is on the same row as their partner's.

Make one copy of the game sheet for each guest. To play, pass out the game sheet. Players have to pair up the names by drawing lines between them within 5 minutes.

Variation/Tips
❑ Theme the romantically involved so that the list consists only of real life actors/actresses (for movie buffs) or famous couples from literature (for bibliophiles), etc.

❑ To make the game easier, include last names.

❑ If names aren't your crowd's forte, try a different but delicious kind of pairing: peas & carrots, salt & pepper, peaches & cream, strawberries & champagne, gravy & mashed potatoes, bacon & eggs, peanut butter & chocolate, lemon & iced tea, and so on.

GUEST BINGO

A bingo game is generated from facts about your invitees.

When
Coed/all girls bachelorette/shower

How
Make as many photocopies of the Bingo card in the Appendix as you have guests (enlarge the image to make bigger cards). Prepare the cards by writing a fact about an invitee (their career, hobby, favorite food, or names of places they're from or have visited) in each square. Examples: a girl/boy scout, piano player, a webmaster, New York, Hawaii, Toronto, chocolate chip cookies, French fries, etc.

Make each card unique by randomly varying the placement of facts in each square and include some new ones that weren't previously used.

To play, give everybody a handful of candy hearts and a card. To draw a fact, the host goes to players one at a time asking them to reveal one of the squares that applies to them (that player also gets to place a candy on that square). For example, the selected player says she was once a girl scout. Any other player who shares this fact announces so, "Oh, I was a girl scout too!" and gets to place a candy on their card's "girl scout" square.

Play continues with another player revealing an applicable fact until everybody's had a round. The first person to place their beans in 5 squares in a row horizontally, diagonally, or vertically calls out "Bingo" and wins a prize.

Variation/Tips
❑   To make this even more challenging, require players to fill in all their squares (a "black out") before they're allowed to declare "Bingo."

HANDFUL OF CLOTHES

Throw up your hands and grab as many clothespins as you can.

When
Coed/all girls bachelorette/shower/reception

How
According to Mexican tradition, each pin you grab in this game represents clothing you've hung over the years. Prepare a clothes hanger by clipping clothespins along the hanger until it's completely covered.

Players take turns going one at a time. The object is to use one hand only to remove and hold as many pins as possible from the hanger (use the other hand to hold the hanger). A player's turn ends when they drop a pin. Write down each player's total when they've had their limit.

Replenish the hanger with pins and let the next player do their turn. Everybody puts their hands together for the victor who held the most number of pins.

Variation/Tips
❑   Instill a time limit to increase excitement in the competition.

HONEYMOON HOOTS

Comments that predict the betrothed's passionate honeymoon night exclamations.

When
Coed/all girls shower

How
Assign someone to discretely write down the Bride-to-be's comments as she opens her gifts.

After the last gift is opened, tell the Bride that legend has it her comments during the gift opening will predict what she'll cry out during her first night of matrimonial bliss. Then read the comments back to her. Typical expressions: "Wow, this is big!" and "What is it?" and "Oh, this is just too cute!" suddenly become a whole lot funnier.

This non-competitive activity is played purely for laughs.

Variation/Tips
❑ Record the session on audio cassette. Edit the funniest comments onto another tape and play them for reception guests after a brief explanation.

❑ If the Bride isn't the effusive type, record comments uttered by your attendees. They'll be just as funny.

❑ Here's a variation to include party attendees: give each guest a piece of paper and pencil, have them place the paper on the floor and ask them to trace their hand on the paper without bending their knees. Record anything uttered. When they're finished, tell them their comments are predictions of what the Bride is going to say on her honeymoon night and read some of sentences back. "I can't reach it!" and "Am I doing this right?" are common results.

I WISH

Wishful pre-marital thinking.

When
Coed/all girls bachelorette/shower

How
Give each guest 10 jelly beans. Gather players around one small cooking pot. Players take turns declaring a goal they wish they can accomplish or perform before they get married. Anybody who has attained that wish throws a bean into the pot. The wish maker then collects the beans.

Here's how the game plays out: one player begins with "I wish to... before getting married." while filling in the blank, for example, "spend a summer in Europe." Any player who has completed said aspiration must throw one of their jelly beans into the pot. (Any player who has not executed that feat does nothing.) The wishful thinker then collects all the beans (if any) from the pot. Next person states their wish.

Play continues until everybody has made an "I wish" declaration. (Married players state a feat they wish had they accomplished before marrying.)

The one with the most jelly beans by the end of a round wins, though, it's the revelation of people's dreams and accomplishments that's far more intriguing.

Variation/Tips
❑ Devote a couple minutes in between "I wish" declarations to discussing the last player's aspiration, if desired.
❑ Substitute plastic wedding rings for jelly beans.
❑ If your players are bold, try "I Never." Participants take turns declaring something they have never done, such as "I never got naked in a pool before." Anybody who has tosses in a bean. An enjoyable game depends on your players having a similar sense of openness. Curb teasing to keep the game enjoyable for all.

IF

Guests pick each other's brains to determine who's on their mind.

When
Coed/all girls bachelorette/shower

How
This game is most appropriate for a group of closely knit friends. Each guest picks another guest to keep in mind, but doesn't tell anybody who they've chosen. One player stands up and the rest of the group take turns guessing who the player is thinking about by asking "If" questions.

These questions should run along the lines of, "If she were a cocktail, what cocktail would she be?", "If she were a fruit, what would she be?", "If she were a fabric, what kind of fabric would she be?", "If she were a dress, what kind of dress would she be?", etc.

Once the player answers a question, the asker can take a guess at who it might be. If the asker is wrong, another participant asks a question and makes their guess. The participant who can determine who the player is thinking about wins that round. The game continues with the next player who gets bombarded with questions.

Variation/Tips
❑ A variation is to let one asker continue pitching questions until they're able to determine who the introspective one has in mind. Count the number of questions asked. The person who got revealed then becomes the questioner with a fresh player. Player who solves the mystery with the least number of questions wins.
❑ If guests are having a hard time, advise them to craft questions to help them eliminate choices and build upon an answer together.
❑ Make players draw names so that everybody is randomly assigned a partner to keep in mind.

KISS & MAKE-UP

Blindfolded guests try their hand at dolling-up the Bride.

When
All girls bachelorette/shower

How
The Bride has to be a good sport to sit for this make over. Prepare a collection of make-up supplies: lipstick, eye shadow, blush, lipstick pencil, foundation, powder, lip gloss, etc. (Do not use mascara.) Write out the names of your beauty supply on separate slips of paper and put in a paper bag.

The number of participants is limited to the number of cosmetics you have on hand. Each player draws a paper slip with a beauty product written on it and that's what they'll apply. The guest is blindfolded and she must put the Bride's face on. Remove the blindfold after the guest is finished with their item.

When all your make-up artists have done a turn, give the Bride a mirror. The artist who uses the war paint the neatest is your winner. Though, this game is less about winning, more about laughing.

Variation/Tips
❑ Divide attendees into small teams and provide them with a bag of make-up. Each group has 8 minutes to create the worst make-up job ever on a member of the team. The Bride-to-be awards the team with the worst looking model a prize.

❑ Ask the Groom to sit in place of the Bride.

LOVE SONGS

Match couples to their wedding song.

When
Coed bachelorette/shower

How
Give each couple, including the Bride, an index card, a copy of the guest list, and a pen. Ask them to write on the index card the name of the song played for their first dance at their wedding reception. If couples can't recall that tune, ask them to write down "their" song, the one that was special to them when they were courting.

Collect the cards. Read out each title and let players ponder and write the name of the melody next to the couple they believe the ditty belongs to on their copy of the guest list. After everyone has written down their answers, read out each title again and ask the matching couple to identify themselves.

Players get a point for each correct answer. Those who correctly matched the Bride's song gets three points. Player with the highest score takes the prize.

Variation/Tips
❑ For unhitched attendees or those not currently in a relationship, they should write their favorite love song.
❑ When most guests do not know each other, provide name tags to make the guessing easier.
❑ Reserve this game for play at the later part of the party. Guests may be able to make more educated guesses after they have had a chance to familiarize themselves with one another.

Sniffing out the spice of life.

When
Coed/all girls bachelorette/shower

How
Prepare 10 small tea cups or bowls with 10 different spices (choose ground spices like cinnamon, brown sugar, turmeric, cloves, etc. so that they're more difficult to recognize). Affix a number to each cup or bowl.

Pass the seasonings around so that every guest gets a whiff. They should jot down the spice number and what they think the spice is on a card. After everyone has cast their guesses, announce the spices and declare the person with the most accurate answers the winner.

Variation/Tips
❑ Purchase 10 spice bottles and wrap paper around each bottle so that no one can see the original label. Write a number on each bottle and proceed with play. When it's time to announce the spices, say the number on the bottle and unwrap the paper to reveal the spice's identity. After the game is over, put the caps back on the spice jar and award the collection as a prize to the winner or give to the Bride as a gift.

Bride tracks down the mistress of the nightie.

When
All girls bachelorette/shower

How
Tell each guest ahead of time (like in the invitation) to bring her favorite sleepwear for a game. As ladies arrive, clip each article of bedtime clothing to a clothesline with a number.

To play, have everybody, including the Bride, write down who she thinks is the owner of which lingerie based on her impressions. Reward the master sleuth who answers with the most correct matches.

Variation/Tips
☐ Make the Bride the only player who has to guess.

☐ To up the stakes, make the Bride perform a penalty for each incorrect answer she gives.

☐ If a player's preference is to sleep in the nude, feel free to clip just a number to the clothesline!

☐ Instead of sleepwear, ask guests to bring a clean pair of undies or bra.

☐ If you prefer, display each garment in its own clear plastic bag.

☐ If your crowd is bold and willing, make it a coed gathering and require the guys to bring their clean jammies or underwear too.

SHOE-IN

Comparing similarities between sole mates.

When
Coed bachelorette/shower/reception

How
Seat the Bride and Groom back to back on chairs so they can't see the other during this game of footsie. Instruct them to take off both their shoes and trade one with their partner so that each person is holding one of their own shoe and one of their beloved's.

The host reads a list of comparative questions one by one that the couple have to raise their footgear in answer. For example, "Who tells the most jokes?" If the Bride's answer is herself, then she holds up her shoe. If her answer is her partner, then she raises his shoe. Ditto for the Groom, he answers the same question at the same time with his shoe (him) or her shoe (her).

A good time is afoot when their shoes don't match up. Try to tailor queries to the Bride and Groom's idiosyncrasies. Refer to the Appendix for additional questions. At the end of the game, tell the couple the number of times they put their best foot forward with matching shoes.

Variations/Tips
❏ Instead of shoes, give them each a separate Bride and Groom cake topper, or stuffed animals (two pigs and two hens, etc.), or use your imagination. Just be sure to obtain two of each set.

❏ A fun twist: award the couple a can of food for each matching answer they give. For each mismatched answer, remove the label from the can then give them the label-less can. Or, instead of food, reward the couple with a dollar for each matched answer, for each mismatched answer a dollar goes to a local charity.

❏ Try different pairings: in-laws, siblings, mom-daughter, etc.

❏ Give everyone at the party a pink square (the Bride) and a blue square of paper (the Groom). Everybody answers at the same time with the couple. Since this is just a way to include everyone on the fun, no score keeping is needed for the group, just the Bride and Groom only.

SOCK IT TO ME

Get footloose with some nice packages.

When
Coed/all girls bachelorette/shower

How
Gather 8 to 10 items that are pertinent to the honeymoon: a corkscrew, sun block, hotel key, etc. and put each item in a clean white athletic sock. Tie it closed and clip a number to the sock.

Instruct gamers the object is to correctly identify the item in each sock by touch, but they can't use their hands, they must use their feet!

A player should pass a sock (by foot) on to another guest after they've given it the once over. Guests follow in each other's footsteps by writing down each sock's number and what they think is in that sock.

After everyone has socked away their answers, pour out the contents. The one most in touch with their feet (has the most correct answers) triumphs.

Variations/Tips
❑   For a racier game, try using innocuous items that could be mistaken for marital aids (a zucchini, a bracelet, a travel size tube of toothpaste, etc.).

❑   If both bucks and hens are attending the event, prepare 6 items that women typically use and 6 items men typically use. Give the 6 women-items to the men to identify and 6 man-items to the gals and see who's more accurate. Woman items could be a tampon, pantyhose, lipstick, etc. Man items might be an athlete's cup, an electric razor, a tie clip, etc.

❑   To prevent players from dragging their feet during the game, set a time limit of 10 seconds to feel up each sock.

Find out if they can give as good as they get.

When
Coed/all girls bachelorette/shower

How
Pass out yarn, telling players to take as much or little as they feel they need. Explain you will tell them what the yarn is for after they've clamed their share. Invariably, a guest insists on asking how much to take. Simply reply, "Not too much and not too little."

Once everybody has some yarn, instruct players to take turns standing up and talking about him/herself while wrapping the yarn around their index finger. The length of yarn determines how long they must talk about themselves. They can not stop until they've finished wrapping all the yarn up. However, the first fact should be somehow related to the Bride or Groom (such as how the speaker met the Bride, or how she helped the Bride name her pet goldfish, etc.). Give a reward to the one who took the most yarn and was a good enough sport to keep talking the entire time.

Variation/Tips
❑ Instead of yarn, pass out toilet paper or paperclips. For every clip or square of paper a player holds in their hand, that player shares an equal number of facts about him/herself.

❑ Substitute yarn with small candies like M&Ms® or jelly beans. Admonish the group not to eat the candies. Each sweet they have in their hand requires the revelation of one bit of personal trivia.

❑ Change the rule of revealing facts about oneself to revealing only facts about the Bride (or Groom). Each fact has to be unique.

❑ Instead of facts, ask players for one bit of marriage advice for each item in their hand.

❑ Another twist, when using yarn or toilet paper, is that whoever has a length that is closest to the diameter of the Bride's bust, waist, and/or thigh wins a goodie.

SUPER PURSE

Players take a load off and weigh in.

When
All girls bachelorette/shower

How
Put a scale in the center of the room. Ask each guest to bring her purse up and place it on the scale. Announce its weight to the group and record each weigh-in. After all weights are recorded, award a prize to the owner of the heaviest and the lightest bag.

Variation/Tips
❑ To adapt this game to men, weigh their wallets on a food or postage scale (anything that measures in ounces).

❑ Send guests on a scavenger type hunt through their own purse. Prepare a list of items commonly and not so commonly found in a purse, ranging from most common to least common in the list. Announce items on the list one by one, asking people to set the item on the table in front of them when they find it in their handbag. Easy items might be a key, lipstick, tissue, bobby pins, breath mints, then progress to slightly more obscure items like a sewing kit, full-sized brush, crackers, postage stamp, unpaid bill, and the downright unusual such as a stapler, marble, flashlight, and toothbrush. It's highly entertaining to see the oddball things that women carry. There's usually at least one packrat with just tons of strange stuff.

❑ A variation on the scavenger hunt is to announce, one at a time, a handful of common items and award a prize to the person who can dig it out of their handbag first.

❑ Another way to play at the reception: announce a few rare items one at a time and award a prize (or the table centerpiece) to the person who retrieves it from their purse (or wallet) first.

TIDY WHITIES

Guess white from wrong in a bag.

When
Coed/all girls bachelorette/shower

How
Before guests arrive, fill individual clear sandwich bags with half a cup of each of the following: flour, cornstarch, sugar, powered sugar, salt, baking powder, baking soda, cream of tartar, and powdered milk. Number each bag and keep a master key of each bag's contents.

Let guests fondle and examine each whitewashed baggie. They are not allowed to open the bags. Everybody writes down what white stuff they think is in each bag as white lightning strikes. After guests have written down their great white hope, you read the master key to the group. The victor is the player with the white touch.

Variation/Tips
❑ Instead of filling bags with items from the pantry, fill bags with cleansing powders such as laundry detergent, countertop scrubbing powders, powdered bleach, etc. When numbering each bag, clearly mark with "Cleansing Powder!!" After the game, return the powders to their original containers or dispose of safely.

TO BE A GOOD SPOUSE

Friends provide humorous or blush inducing advice to the marriage-bound couple.

When
Coed/all girls bachelorette/shower

How
Every attendee receives two index cards and a pen. Each person is to fill in the following sentences, each on a separate card: "To be a good husband, John, you should..." and "To be a good wife, Jane, you should..."

After everyone has penned their pearl of wisdom, the Groom collects his advice cards and the Bride collects her advice cards. They switch bags. Each take turns reading their friend's advisories aloud to their significant other.

Encourage guests to be clever. Depending on the group, counsel can aim to provoke giggles, "To be a good husband, John, you should give Margo a dollar." or flush the couple's cheeks, "To be a good wife, Jane, you should put away those whips."

Variation/Tips
❑ It's always an option to set boundaries like "keep it clean" or "keep it nice" before commencing play.

WHO WOULD YOU DO?

Honor the Bride's farewell to bachelorhood by discussing
fictional conquests.

When
Coed/all girls bachelorette

How
Players take turns posing a hypothetical to the group, "Who would you
rather sleep with, X or Y?" inserting the names of celebrities or
fictional characters.

This game is more fun when both choices are especially appealing--or
unappealing for that matter. Like "Who would you rather sleep with, a
Policeman or Fireman?" There are no winners or losers, just a
provocative discourse.

Variation/Tips
❑ A tamer alternative is to take turns posing 50-50 quandaries to
each other, like "Wine or soda?" and "Sit com or drama?" See
additional 50-50 questions in the Appendix.

MEMORY/WORD GAMES

BARING ALL

Trivia answers gradually disrobe a strong and silent type.

When
All girls bachelorette/shower

How
Before playing, prepare a life-sized cardboard silhouette of a man. Cut out an appropriately sized man's face from a magazine and tape to the cardboard head. Write "No peeking!" in the groin area. Dress this one-dimensional man to party in a g-string and pants, belt, socks, T-shirt, outer shirt/jacket, tie, sunglasses, and a hat.

You'll need to compose at least 10 trivia questions about the Bride and Groom (check out the Appendix for inspiration). There should be more questions than items of clothing on your party dude.

To play, randomly call on guests to answer a trivia question about the engaged couple. If you have a large group of players, let the majority come to a consensus before electing a person to answer.

If the player answers correctly, she is allowed to peel off one piece of clothing from the corrugated guy. If she's incorrect, clothing stays on.

The game ends when only the g-string remains. Leave it up to guests to resist temptation to look further.

Variations/Tips
❑ Instead of using a cardboard cut-out, borrow a set of clothes from the Groom and stuff with gifts for the Bride. Toilet paper can fill out the chest, rolls of foil or plastic wrap make the arms and legs. Two mixing bowls fitted together create a head. The betrothed gets to undo one piece of clothing for each trivia question correctly answered by the group.

❑ Sizzle up the game by asking a male friend to volunteer as a real-life strong and silent type. Play proceeds as normal.

BEST FRIEND VS. THE GROOM

The Bride's best friend and her intended speculate on the Bride's fancy.

When
Coed bachelorette/shower

How
Send the Bride's closest friend and her future spouse out of the room for this contest. Ask the Bride to choose one personal preference over another in eleven 50-50 questions like, "Eat in or eat out?", "Pen or pencil?" Write down the Bride's answers.

Have the close friend and Groom return to the room. Ask them the same 50-50 questions, but their job is to correctly predict the Bride's answers. Alternate who responds first. Reveal which person got it right after every question and keep track. Whoever gets the most matches is victor. See the Appendix for more 50-50 questions.

Variation/Tips
❑ Expand the game to include more players. Send the Bride out of the room first. Have all participants, including the Groom and best friend, write their predictions of the Bride's answers to the 50-50 questions down. Then, have the Bride come back into the room and answer the 50-50 questions. Players check off any matches. Most correct matches wins.

❑ Turn the tables and shower the Groom with some attention. Have the Bride and her best friend try to predict the fiancé's answers.

CHECK OUT THE BRIDE

Here comes the Bride, all dressed in... what?

When
Coed/all girls bachelorette/shower

How
This should be played shortly after the last guest has arrived. Let the Bride mingle for 10 minutes then have the Bride step out of the room (or behind a screen).

Give each guest paper and pencil, tell guests the game is to remember as many details as they can about the Bride by answering a list of ten questions that you have prepared ahead of time. Some possibilities:

- ❑ What color was her shirt?
- ❑ Did she have earrings on?
- ❑ Was she wearing a watch?
- ❑ What did she have in her hair?
- ❑ What color were her shoes?
- ❑ What kind of shoes was she wearing?
- ❑ Was she wearing any perfume?
- ❑ How many buttons were on her shirt?

Once all players have written down their answers, the Bride steps back into the room and goes over the correct answers. Players place a checkmark by their correct answers and add them up. The eagle-eyes with the most checkmarks wins.

Variations/Tips
❑ Announce to attendees that they're going to play a memory game. Have the Bride walk around the room with a baking sheet filled with a variety of kitchen items. Provide pad and paper to each guest. The Bride leaves the room with the items. Give players 5 minutes to list everything they can remember--not of the items on baking sheet, but the clothing on the Bride!

When the Bride returns, award the player with the most correct number of details. When people have settled back down, tell everyone there's a second part to the game. They now have an additional 5 minutes to remember and list everything that was on the baking sheet!

ETIQUETTE

Hilarious answers to outrageous wedding etiquette questions.

When
Coed/all girls bachelorette/shower

How
Before guests arrive, write one etiquette question for each attendee on individual index cards. Have an equal number of blank cards ready. Below are sample questions, precede each with, "What do you do if..."

❑   You see the Groom has his fly down during the ceremony?
❑   You're allergic to the fish being served at the reception?
❑   The best man comes down with food poisoning the morning of the wedding?
❑   The Bride is getting drunk on champagne?
❑   You accidentally mash half of the wedding cake with your camera?

The more whoppers you can come up with, the funnier this game becomes.

Randomly give each guest an etiquette question and blank card. Tell them to write their sincere answer to the assigned question on the blank card.

Collect the question and answer cards, putting the question card in one paper bag, and all the answer cards in another.

Have each guest randomly draw a question card and answer card and read them aloud to the group. For example, one question and answer pair might go like this, "What do you do if the Groom has his fly down during the ceremony? Eat around the fish, then push it around your plate and hope nobody notices."

Read however many Q&As time/enthusiasm allows for. See the Appendix for more disasters.

Variation/Tips
❑   If appropriate, save a few gems to share at the reception.

FAMILY CIRCLE

Memorizing relations is the name of the game.

When

Coed/all girls bachelorette/shower

How

Learning and recalling the names of extended relations is a special skill to be cultivated. Here's a game to get practicing for the wedding.

Everybody sits in a circle and one person at a time introduces him or herself by saying their first name and favorite fruit or hobby that starts with the first initial of their name. Examples: "Hi, I'm Marc and I like mountaineering." or "I'm Annie and I like apricots."

Once a complete round has been made, the first person to do their introduction attempts to remember as many name-fruit/hobby combinations as they can. The name caller with the most correct number of pairings can claim a prize.

Variation/Tips

❑ Another way to play: guests state their name and a fictional gift they brought: "My name is Lori and I brought a luscious lamp."

❑ In lieu of making a whole round before reciting the combinations, gradually add on introductions. After the first guest introduces herself, the guest to her right adds their name/gift then repeats the previous guest's introduction, "My name is Faith and I brought a fancy fan, Lori brought a luscious lamp." The next person starts with their name/gift, repeats Faith's, then Lori's name/gift and so on. The game proceeds in clockwise fashion, but players have to recall in counter-clockwise direction. If a player forgets someone in the chain, play continues on to the next person.

❑ A slightly simpler variation is to have guests state a wedding or bridal shower related word (instead of their name and association), such as gown, church, limousine, or reception, etc. The next guest adds her own word, then repeats the previous guests' word, etc.

GET THE PICTURE

Everyone contributes to this pretty as a picture moment.

When
Coed/all girls bachelorette/shower

How
Play this sitting down or standing up, it doesn't matter, just gather everyone into a circle. This word game begins with either the Bride or Groom's name. Each player will progressively add a descriptive detail about what the subject is doing and where while repeating the previously added detail. A picture perfect scenario emerges as the group gradually creates this run-on sentence.

How a game might go: Start with Jack the Groom. First player says "Jack in his undies." The second player might say "Jack in his white undies." And third player says "Jack in his white undies looking at his platinum watch." Next player says "Jack in his white undies looking at his platinum watch outside Jane's door." Then, "Jack in his white undies looking at his platinum watch outside Jane's bedroom door." Then, "Jack in his white undies looking at his platinum watch outside Jane's bedroom door with a dozen red roses." And so on.

This game is less a challenge on memory, more about being creative together. Players should help one another keep track of the chain. End the fairy tale when everybody has had a turn or the sentence reaches a satisfying conclusion.

Variation/Tips
❏ Once players get the hang of this and want to play more, encourage them to concoct more vivid and funny scenarios around the Bride and/or Groom.
❏ You can also expand the subject to include any members of the wedding party who are game to participate.
❏ Write down the final sentence for the happy couple to keep in a memory album.

HAPPILY EVER AFTER

A random story about married life.

When
Coed/all girls bachelorette/shower/reception

How
Prepare a brief story that predicts life in the future for Mr. and Mrs. Doe, then take out key words like "They will have ? children whose names are ? and ?." (Or, borrow our sample story from the Appendix if you're short on time.)

Without telling guests what the story is about, ask participants to help fill in the details by shouting out a random number, that number of names, and other missing nouns, verbs, or adjectives until the tall tale is filled in. Read the completed story out loud for the group's enjoyment.

Variations/Tips
❑ Vary the subject of the story according to the occasion. If it's a bachelorette party, for example, the story might be a wicked fictional tale from his wild past. A story about how the couple met would be appropriate for the reception.

IN BED

Dreaded household chores take on new meanings.

When
Coed/all girls bachelorette/shower

How
Everybody gets a scrap of paper to jot down a household chore they hate to do. The chore has to be written like this, "I hate... because..." For example, "I hate taking out the trash at night because it's a long cold walk."

Do not tell guests what the sayings are really for until everybody has finished writing down their chore and exchanged it with someone else.

Now tell guests they have to read the person's gripe aloud for the group, but substitute the word "sex" for the chore. So the example now becomes, "I hate sex at night because it's a long cold walk."

Variation/Tips
❑ A popular variation is to pass out fortune cookies and have everyone take turns reading their fortune aloud, but adding the words "in bed" at the end of the sentence. A typical one might read, "You will travel to exotic places... in bed."

❑ Instead of chores, players write a 25 word or less classified ad for something they'd like to sell. When they're done, the ad writers replace each mention of the item with their name and read the new classified to the group. If the attendees are mostly couples, they should replace the item with their partner's name in the ad.

LIKE MINDED

Players free associate words to see how many match the
Bride's associations.

When
Coed/all girls bachelorette/shower

How
Prepare a list of ten random words before playing. Someone other
than the Bride should prepare this list because the Bride has to be one
of the players during the game. Suggested words: love, cake,
diamond, husband, faithful, flowers, dog, in-laws, honeymoon, bed,
secret, babies.

Give each player a pad of paper and pen. They should number the first
ten lines, one through ten. Announce that this is a free association
game. They should write down whatever word comes to their mind
first after they hear a word read off the list.

Once all the words have been read, tell players that the player with
the most reaction words that match the Bride's reaction words wins
this game. The Bride reads off her list and everybody checks their list
to determine who is most like minded.

Variation/Tips
❑   If no one's word association matched the Bride's association for
    the same word, expand the rule so that any word written on their
    list matching any word written by the Bride scores.

LOVE LETTER

Sweet nothings penned by party invitees.

When
Coed/all girls bachelorette/shower

How
Instruct the group that they're being drafted to help the Groom write a love letter, but each person gets to write only one sentence.

Start out with one piece of paper on a clipboard with the words "Dear Jane" on it. Give this to the first player and have them write the second line under the first. The first player now must fold down the first line ("Dear Jane") so that it's hidden underneath the paper and pass it onto the second player.

This second player adds his or her line and folds down the last line (the one before theirs) and passes on the clipboard. After the mash note has made a round (or 2 if the group is less than 10 people), read the letter out loud for the Bride and company.

Variation/Tips
❑   If the letter's tone is appropriate and funny enough, read it at the reception.
❑   Change the love letter to a story of how the Bride and Groom met. Instead of guests writing sentences, they're instructed to fill in parts of the sentence (one guest per blank). For example, The Bride's name is ... The Groom's name is ... They met at .... in .... The Groom's first thought was ..... And the Bride said .... On their first date, they ate .... at ..... etc.

MEAT AND POTATOES

Identify the missing ingredient in these comfort food recipes.

When
Coed/all girls bachelorette/shower

How
Before playing, type up 10 simple recipes for basic dishes like tuna casserole, brownies, potato salad, spaghetti, etc. (or they could be for the Bride and Groom's favorite dishes) and randomly omit one ingredient per recipe. Don't forget to X out references to the missing ingredient from the recipe instructions as well. Make one copy per guest and staple each set together.

Give one set of recipes to each player. Players must write what they think the missing ingredient is next to each recipe. Solicit a couple of guesses for each dish before providing the answer.

Crown the player with the most correct answers as your master of domestic science. As a bonus, let everybody keep their collection of meal-time favorites.

Variation/Tips
❑ To provide a greater challenge, substitute a couple ethnic food recipes.
❑ Instead of comfort food recipes, use mixed cocktail drink recipes.

MEMORY LANE

Stroll down memory lane with fond stories about the Bride-to-be.

When
All girls shower

How
Guests sit in a circle and take turns sharing a cherished or funny anecdote about the engaged or recall the first time they met her. Players vote for their favorite story afterwards.

Variation/Tips

❑ Prompt tongue-tied speakers with suggestions on other topics to elicit additional entertaining stories: how she first heard of her engagement, how she decided on her gift, a time they fought and made-up, the first time she met her fiancé, when she first knew that boyfriend was going to become the fiancé, etc.

❑ In the invitations, ask guests to bring a prop to illustrate their memory involving the Bride. The prop could be a souvenir, ticket stub, or any memento from the story. Attendees shouldn't be expected to weave a lengthy tale, but a brief explanation behind the prop will be sufficient.

RECIPES FOR LOVE

Relationship chefs share their wacky/teary/racy recipes for wedded bliss.

When
Coed/all girls bachelorette/shower

How
Give everybody an index card and pen. Ask each person to write down a recipe for joyful matrimony that's customized to the engaged couple.

Tell the scribes they have 5 to 10 minutes to cook up a storm. Depending on individuals in the crowd, this could be written for laughs, completely sincere, or erotically charged. Encourage wit and imagination.

After everyone has put the finishing touches on their recipes, collect them. The Bride (and Groom, if he's playing) draws one card at a time to read aloud. The Bride has to try to name the cook who concocted each recipe. Everybody's a winner in this game.

Variation/Tips
❏ Make the Bride/Groom perform a penalty if they're unable to accurately match the recipe to the guest who penned it.
❏ Feel free to issue some boundaries on the recipes before any writing commences, especially in mixed company.

SWEET STORIES

Weave a juicy tale about the betrothed using candy bars.

When
Coed/all girl's bachelorette/shower

How
Prepare a baking sheet with 20 to 25 different kinds of candy: 100 Grand®, Snickers®, Kisses®, Big Hunk®, KitKat®, Now & Later®, Jolly Rancher®, Runts®, Pop Rocks®, etc. Cover the items with a dishtowel. Divide players into groups of no more than 5 members. You'll want a minimum of two groups.

Go to the first group and expose the randy candy to them for 30 seconds. Advise players to look carefully. Then tell them they have 10 minutes to write a story about the Bride and Groom (how they met or how they planned the wedding, etc.) while incorporating as many candy names they can remember.

Let the first group start, then show the candy tray to the next group and repeat with remaining groups. Once time is up, each group assigns a person to read their story out loud. A sweet story might read like this: When Jane first met Jolly Rancher John, she thought he was a Big Hunk. Even though neither had 100 Grand, they traded many Kisses Now and Later... etc. The Bride-to-be gets to determine the winning story.

Variations/Tips
❑ Instead of candy bars, substitute household products like Life® cereal, Secret® deodorant, Sparkle® towels, Cheer® detergent, etc. Present the products in a laundry basket to the Bride as a gift after the stories are read. (Or award the products as prizes to players.)
❑ Collect all the stories and place in a memory book for the Bride.
❑ A different sugar session: wrap each candy in white paper, write a marriage riddle on the wrapping. Players get their answer by unwrapping the candy. For example: Things you shouldn't tell your spouse. Answer: Whoppers®. Give each player a wrapped sweet. Taking turns, players read out their riddle, say their answer, then unwrap the candy to confirm. If correct, player wins the candy. More Q&A: What the Bride likes to call her Groom: Big Hunk; Needed to cover wedding expenses: PayDay®; What lovers trade freely: Kisses®; When a couple fight, they need to...: Take 5®; What the Bride & Groom expect on their Honeymoon: Skor®; When the couple should start saving for retirement: Now & Later.

WEDDING SCRAMBLE

Wedding words give birth to wee ones.

When
Coed/all girls bachelorette/shower

How
Prepare a list of five wedding-related words, such as commitment, champagne, honeymoon, engagement, and marriage. Give everyone a pad and pencil. Players have to use the letters in a given word to form as many new words as possible. The new words must be three letters or longer to count. Allow players three minutes per root word.

For example, read off the word "limousine," and give players three minutes to deliver words like "nose" and "mouse." Read off the next root word from your list and wait for the allotted time before advancing. Each letter in a root word can only be used once.

At the end of this bridal boggle, have a player read off the new words they've "unscrambled" from the original word. The other players need to listen because if they have the same word, they (and the person reading the word) have to cross the repeated word off their list. Every remaining player takes a turn reading off what words they have left on their list. Continue with the next root word. Everybody gets one point for any unique words remaining in their lists. Whoever has the most number of points wins.

Variations/Tips
❏ Up the list to 10 if the group is especially adept at this game. Additional words you might use: banquet, betrothal, diamonds, and mother-in-law.

WHAT'S IN A NAME

The name of love put into words.

When
Coed/all girls bachelorette/shower

How
Give each guest paper and a pen. Instruct participants to write down the first name of the Bride and Groom down the left edge of the paper. Now, everyone has three minutes to write as many wedding themed words as they can that start with each letter in the couple's names.

Say the Groom's name is Jon, the row with the letter "J" might have "joy," "join," "Juno" (goddess of marriage), "jolly," etc. When time is up, guests take turns reading what they have for each letter. If another guest or more has the same word, everybody has to cross that word off their list for that letter. Each unique word a guest has remaining (after all words have been read aloud) earns one point. The player with the most points earns the championship title.

Variation/Tips
❑ Instead of writing the matrimony-bound couple's names vertically, write both their first and last names across the top of the paper. Now, see how many words (of three letters or more) guests can create from the available letters in three minutes. For example, the names John and Jane offer two J's and two N's, one O and one A, etc. Like the original game, guests cross off words that others have duplicated. Award points by the length of the word: a three letter word gets 1 point, four letter word gets 2 points, a five letter word scores 3 points, etc.

ACTIVE GAMES

A TYPICAL MORNING

The Groom's hands come to life as he enacts a typical morning.

When
Coed bachelorette/reception

How
Prepare a table with props from the Groom's morning rituals: shaver, shaving cream, comb, tie, coffee cup, sugar, toast, newspaper, etc.

Tell the guests and Bride something like this: "Jane, ever since you came into John's life, John changed into a better man. To show you how he's improved, we're going to do a dramatic re-enactment of a typical morning for John before he met you."

Stand the Groom behind the table, facing the audience, and his hands behind his back. His best man stands behind him, sticking his arms and hands out from under the Groom's arms so that the best man's hands act as the Groom's hands. Start the skit with an intro, "This is John, before he met Jane." and let his "hands" wave hello.

Continue with, "John's very slow to wake up in the mornings." The best man gently slaps John's face to "wake" him. "That's why he really needs his morning coffee." The best man messily makes coffee and feeds the Groom his java. Continue narrating his attempts to eat breakfast and don a tie for work. Conclude with, "Now you see why, Jane, we're really glad you're marrying John!"

The best man's dramatic hand flourishes and inevitable sloppiness from his limited vision make the show funnier. Try to personalize and rehearse the skit in advance with the best man.

Variation/Tips
❑ Instead of narrating, interview the Groom on his daily routines. This is a fun way for guests to learn more about him. "Tell us how you prepare for the morning? What do you make for breakfast? Do you wear a tie? How long is the commute to work? What do you do at work?" The Best Man does his best to go through the motions with his hands.

❑ Use a tablecloth or garbage bag as a bib to protect his clothes.

ASK FOR HER HAND

Can the Groom or Bride recognize their beloved among strangers?

When
Coed bachelorette/shower/reception

How
Blindfold the Groom, then select 10 female players. Have the Bride join the players and form a line. The blindfolded Groom must locate his Bride by a handshake.

Guide him down the lineup and let him shake hands with each woman without speaking to her. When he thinks he's in the right hands, remove the blindfold.

If the Groom's first guess was wrong, the women change places in the lineup and the Groom goes a second round. If he's wrong again, hand down a penalty to the Groom.

Variations/Tips
- Switch roles and let the Bride try her hand at finding her love.
- Instead of shaking hands, the guesser might touch the lineup's calves, buns, or ears. Or, have the lineup kiss the Bride on the cheek one by one and see if she recognizes her lover's lips.
- For laughs, switch out the Bride (if the Groom correctly identifies her) with someone else before removing his blindfold. Or, remove her from the lineup before the Groom starts shaking hands, and then reinsert her when he removes his blindfold.
- To prank the Groom, insert the Best Man in the lineup. Or, to really do a number on him, fill the whole lineup with groomsmen and other males from the party while telling him you're selecting beautiful women.
- To include couples, have an equal number of men and women form a line each of boys and girls, hold a bed sheet between the two lines. Players reach over the sheet to shake hands as they go down the line. When a player thinks they've found their partner, they hang onto that hand. No talking allowed. When everybody is paired up, drop the sheet.
- See Up to Snuff for a version that doesn't require physical contact.

BARGAIN WEDDING CAKE

See what's cooking as the Bride-to-be whips up a wedding cake
without the benefit of a recipe.

When
Coed/all girls shower/bachelorette

How
This obviously has to be played in a kitchen. Be sure the pantry is
stocked with ingredients for making a cake: eggs, flour, sugar, baking
powder, milk, vanilla extract, pudding mix, vegetable oil, butter, and
salt. And basic equipment is available: a working oven, 2 cake pans,
bowls, a whisk or electric beaters, measuring cups, measuring spoons.

To give the cake time to bake, play this game first or early in the party
as guests trickle in. Select a guest to be the Bride's helper. Too many
chefs spoil the cake, so stop the well-meaning guest who happens to
be a brilliant cook from stepping in to help the bride.

The Bride has half an hour to mix the cake batter (and frosting if she's
adventurous) by giving verbal directions to her helper. The chef must
also dictate the baking temperature and time. Play other games during
baking. When the confection is finished, gather everybody around and
let them eat cake!

Variations/Tips
- ❑ For the culinary challenged player, set out ingredients she needs
  to make a cake on the kitchen counter and cover with a tablecloth.
  Reveal the ingredients when ready to play. She still has to figure
  out what proportions to put the ingredients in.
- ❑ Make everything but the kitchen sink (garlic, bread crumbs, yeast,
  soda pop, etc.) an available ingredient to the chef.
- ❑ Mix it up by making the Groom and Bride bake separate cakes.
  Vote on whose tastes better.
- ❑ Write down the recipe your honorary baker creates for the
  scrapbook. Record memorable comments made during the tasting.
- ❑ If the bridal baker would prefer to do the measuring and mixing
  herself, select an attentive assistant to write the recipe as she
  goes.

BIG MOUTH

A very sweet mouth off.

When
Coed/all girls bachelorette/shower/reception

How
Prepare a list of 20 famous names. Have several bags of large marshmallows ready. Call up 6 players, or the immediate members of the bridal party (Bride, Groom, groomsmen, bridesmaids).

Everyone begins with one marshmallow in their mouth. The host reads off a famous name and the players take turns repeating the name. Players who succeed in speaking clear enough for the host to understand are given another marshmallow to put in their mouth before saying the next name. Those reduced to incomprehensible blabbermouths are taken out of the game.

The last big mouth standing wins--be sure to announce how many marshmallows total the winner had in their mouth.

Variations/Tips
❑ This game is not recommended for elderly or very young players. Advise players to use caution and play at their own risk.
❑ This game can be used as a penalty for trivia questions the Bride or Groom answers incorrectly. A marshmallow must be inserted in the mouth for every wrong answer given. End the game if the Bride or Groom can not comfortably hold any more.
❑ Instead of famous names, have players say wedding related words like marriage, commitment, monogamy, fidelity, bliss, etc.
❑ A non-marshmallow alternative. Give each player five water crackers to chew and see who is able to whistle first.
❑ This version is less of a mouthful: pull an audience member to be the listener, turn his or her back to the players. Give only one of the six players a hard candy to put in their mouth. Each player takes turns saying the same word. The listener has to accurately pick out the person with the sweet in their mouth. Play again with a new listener, but give every player except one a candy--listener now has to identify the empty mouthed speaker.

CAPTURE THE BRIDE

Groom pays a ransom for the hand of his Bride.

When

Reception

How

This game was likely inspired by the old custom of marriage by bride-napping. At the desired time during the reception, announce to guests that as a test of the Groom's protectiveness and attentiveness, all are invited to try to "kidnap" the Bride.

Anyone who succeeds in sneaking the Bride out of the room can approach the Groom for a ransom (a small wrapped gift) to release the Bride back to him.

Variation/Tips

❑ As an alternative to paying out gifts, the Groom performs a penalty. See the Appendix for ideas.

❑ Announce an end to the game when you want to give the Groom and Bride time to resume their hosting duties. An early end may be necessary to prevent embarrassing the Groom and/or when there are so many successful captures that it disrupts the gathering.

❑ A variation to turn the tables on the Bride: the Bride closes her eyes and the Groom hides himself among guests at the reception. Give the Bride two minutes to locate him. What you don't tell the Bride is that the Groom is in disguise (provide a woman's wig and jacket). If the reception is over 100 guests, add an extra minute per 100 guests to the time limit. If the reception is smaller, reduce the time limit to one minute.

CARVE A CUKE

Wannabe Michelangelos must chisel a manly cucumber.

When
Coed/all girls bachelorette

How
Purchase as many cucumbers (carrots work too) as you have players. You can limit the number so that others can watch, or divide groups into teams of three or four players.

Give each team a knife and a cucumber. Tell players they're to sculpt a life-sized pecker out of that cuke. The Bride and/or Groom give an award to the artist who carved the best rendition.

Variation/Tips
❑ Award the winner with a condom and have them "crown" their winning statue with it--while blindfolded.

CHASTITY

Summon the self-restraint of a virgin to hold one's tongue.

When
Coed/all girls bachelorette/shower

How
Issue each attendee a clothespin (or paperclip or plastic ring or beaded necklace) to wear as they arrive. Greet everyone with the news that they have become virgins upon crossing the home's threshold.

To remain chaste, no one is allowed to say "wedding" during this game. Anyone catching a maiden blurting out the word "wedding" takes their pin. The goal is to collect the most pins.

Those deflowered of their pin may seduce others into uttering the forbidden to reclaim pins. The vigilant individual who nabs someone with more than one pin claims all. In case several players have caught the same act of impropriety, the quickest to stand before the offender gets their pin. At the end of the event, the surviving virgin with the most pins wins a prize.

Variations/Tips
❑ Instead of pins, issue a limited number of party favors. Bestow one present (see Appendix for ideas) for every three arrivals. The game is played the same way. The person who catches someone saying the prohibited word claims all their goods.

❑ Try banishing more than one word.

❑ Give each guest three pins to provide room for mistakes, especially if you want to bar something that's nearly impossible to avoid like the Bride's name, the word "um" or "sweet," etc.

❑ Instead of banning one word, give each guest a name tag with their name and a word they are expressly not allowed to use. If someone collects that sticker, that person adopts the word to their own list of "no-no's."

❑ Instead of forbidding words, make up a rule like "no swearing," or "no crossing your legs" or "no touching your hair" etc.

❑ Require players to pay a compliment to the rule-breaker before taking their token.

THE COLLAGE YEARS

A fuzzy gaze into the couple's future.

When
Coed/all girls bachelorette/shower

How
Divide the gathering into groups of 5 players or less. Give each group three old magazines, a pair of scissors, and a self-sticking photo album page. They will use these materials to construct a collage which depicts their vision of the engaged couple's past, present, or future.

Assign each group a topic they are responsible for depicting: the couple's bachelor years, their courtship, their honeymoon, or their future kids, etc. Give the groups 15 minutes to construct their pages. Pass the collage around for everybody to enjoy. The Bride awards her favorite.

Variation/Tips
❑ Tabloid or gossip magazines are especially rich in pictures and outlandish headlines. Lifestyle, news, and women's magazines are also good resources.
❑ When time's up, don't pass the collage around, have each group pick a member to narrate their vision of life for the happy couple.

CROSSING THE THRESHOLD

Practice carrying the Bride--while wearing her heels!

When
Reception

How
Tell the Groom that now is a good time to practice carrying his new wife across the threshold. The Groom kicks off his shoes and slips into the Bride's shoes. While cradling her in his arms, he must carefully carry her across the length of the dance floor within 10 seconds. If he trips or drops her, he performs a penalty.

Variation/Tips
- ❏ The Groom may choose to carry his Bride piggy back style.
- ❏ Transform this stunt into a race between the Groom/Bride and best man/maid of honor, eliminate the time limit.
- ❏ If the heels are too high or his feet won't fit, forgo making the Groom wear the Bride's shoes.
- ❏ If using a time limit, adjust the time allotted so that it's appropriate to the size of the dance floor.

DOLLAR DANCE

Rent a Bride or Groom.

When
Reception

How
Announce that the Bride and/or Groom are available to do the Dollar Dance (also called a Veil or Honor Dance). Any guest who wishes to dance with the Bride or Groom can do so by giving them at least one dollar bill. Since the dollar dance is another way to shower gifts of cash on the newly married, the dance is not expected to last an entire song, but only part of it.

A bridesmaid or groomsman can help collect the cash in a basket, or provide guests with safety pins to pin the money on the Bride or Groom's clothing.

Variation/Tips
❑ Here's a twist to encourage guests to be generous. In addition to dancing with the Bride or Groom, charitable guests have the privilege of pinning money on the couple's clothing in an amusing way. For example, a donor might pin the Bride's veil into an outrageous upright bouffant, or pin the Groom's sleeve higher so that his tux looks too short. They'll look quite silly by the time the Dollar Dance ends... and that's the point.
❑ Instead of a dance, the Bride may want to offer a kiss for a dollar to her guests.

DRESSING IN THE DARK

Groom rushes to gussy up his mate while blindfolded.

When
Coed bachelorette/shower/reception

How
Beforehand, fill a suitcase with obnoxious and unusual clothing and accessories like bedroom slippers, a scarf or tie, giant sunglasses, a wig, dishwashing gloves, an oversized girdle or lingerie, a baby bib, earmuffs, an apron, etc.

Blindfold the Groom. Tell the couple they've overslept and have two minutes to get dressed for the wedding. The blindfolded player must clothe their non-blindfolded partner with clothing from the suitcase within the time limit. Put the suitcase on a table within arm's reach of the players, but do not open it until the blindfold is on. The player being dressed is not allowed to help.

Count the number of items that get thrown on within those two minutes, announce the grand total at the end.

Variations/Tips
❑ Offer the Bride a turn to dress up her Groom by having them switch roles.

❑ Another way to play is to blindfold both players, give them each a suitcase or laundry bag full of clothing and two minutes to dress themselves with as much clothing as possible.

❑ Tell the players they have to get on a minimum number of clothing, such as eight items within those two minutes, or perform a penalty.

❑ As extra incentive to get the Bride or Groom dressed to the nines, offer a dollar for each piece they can get on.

❑ With additional clothing and props, this game can be expanded to include pairs of guests, such as the best man and maid of honor, both mother-in-laws, or couples, etc.

Gentlemen seek out the owner of a ladies shoe for the privilege of a dance.

When
Reception

How
While the single gals and guys are still gathered from the bouquet/garter toss, ask the bachelors to all step to one side of the dance floor. Have them form a single line along one side of the perimeter and turn away from the ladies standing in the center.

Ask the ladies to remove both of their shoes and leave one in the center of the dance floor. They take their other shoe with them to the side of the dance floor opposite the men. The women hide their shoe behind their back.

Instruct the single guys to turn around, grab a woman's shoe and locate its owner by trying it on the woman he thinks it belongs to. The shoe they grab will determine the woman the men will dance one song with. The ladies cannot assist an errant prince by saying it's not her footwear until she's tried it on.

Once everybody has found their shoe's owner, start music and tell the newly partnered singles to enjoy the dance. This is very effective at getting the singles onto the dance floor early in the evening.

Variation/Tips
❑   Make Cinderella find her prince. This is probably even harder since many men's shoes look alike! Have the men leave a shoe behind and make the ladies locate the owner.

❑   If there are more boys than girls, the Bride and/or her attendants should fill in by dancing with any unattached boys. And if there's more girls than boys, have the Groom and/or his attendants gallantly step in to fill those shoes.

❑   Keep the song short so awkwardly paired couples don't have to suffer too long.

GOSSIP SESSION

Guests practice the gift of gab.

When
Coed/all girls bachelorette/shower

How
Work with the engaged to gather some interesting, hopefully juicy, trivia about all attendees before the gathering. (Do a reality check to ensure the guest will not be offended to have this information become public knowledge.) The fact can be provocative or simply informative, depending on your participants' sense of fun. Then, turn the fact into a question.

Possible trivia questions: What's the name of Jane's Doberman Pincher?, Where did David have his first alcoholic drink?, What did the Groom buy the Bride for their first date?, What's the trick that Amy can do with her tongue?, Who here placed 1st in a local bake-off contest?", etc.

Write down each question on an index card. As each guest arrives, hand him or her one card. Explain they have ten minutes to mingle in the rumor mill and find the answer to the question they've been assigned. At the end of the tongue wagging session, each fact finder takes turns airing the "gossip" they've uncovered.

Variation/Tips
❑ To steer completely clear of any controversial gossip, focus questions on facts and accomplishments that a guest would be proud to share.

❑ Encourage more mingling by giving each guest two or three questions to answer instead of one.

Be the last one standing to avoid getting bumped from the plane.

When
Coed/all girls bachelorette/shower/reception

How
Invite anyone who wants a getaway to come check-in in groups of two. One player is a passenger and their partner acts as carry-on luggage. Give each pair a full-size sheet of newspaper (consists of four pages) to open and lay flat on the floor in front of them, this paper is the plane. Each rider boards with their luggage, in other words, each team steps together onto their paper. Once on board, their feet cannot touch the floor.

Announce the flight is overbooked and people will be bumped so the Bride and Groom can go on their honeymoon. Tell travelers to deplane and fold the sheet in half, then re-board their paper plane. Each pair has to be able to remain on their folded paper for at least 15 seconds to qualify. If luggage or traveler step off their paper during the stand-by period, that pair is out (bumped from the flight).

Proceed to the next round: instruct those remaining to fold the sheet in half again and get back on. Continue halving the paper each round. Keep eliminating pairs who fall out of their plane. Last flyer standing with their bag gets to trip the light fantastic.

Variation/Tips
❑ Staying on the shrinking jetliner will be very difficult by the fourth fold. Wait a little longer to see if any passengers stumble off their paper plane before proceeding to the next fold.
❑ Passengers may attempt to board in sequence. In other words, stagger it so that everybody can observe each team attempt their stand-by period.
❑ Play this fight for flight with individuals the same way you would with pairs. Last person to get bumped wins.
❑ Or, make this a group game: have everyone share one King-sized bed sheet. Keep halving the sheet until there's one person remaining on it.
❑ Since the Bride and Groom mainly serve as observers in this game, they should use this opportunity to rest and eat.

KISS THE PIG

A pig tells you where to plant one.

When
Coed bachelorette

How
Players sit in a circle, alternating boy-girl. The host stands in the center with a small plush pig toy. Holding the pig in front of her, the host says, "I kiss the pig on the cheek." and kisses it lightly on the cheek.

The host then passes the pig to a player and they have to do the same, then pass it on. The only rule here is that each guest must pick a unique body part to smooch. Once the pig has gone full circle, the host announces that each player must now kiss the person to their left on the same place they kissed the pig!

Variations/Tips
❑ To draw out this saucy game a little further, have guests do the kissing in turn so that everyone gets to enjoy the exchange.

OH DARLING!

Husband and wife practice addressing their better half.

When
Coed bachelorette/shower/reception

How
Clear obstacles from your playing field, a ten-foot square such as the dance floor at a reception is ideal. Blindfold both the Bride and Groom and take them to opposite corners of the square.

Like "Marco-Polo," the Groom must call out "Darling" (or "wife" or "dumpling") and the Bride must answer "Sweetheart" (or "Husband" or "hey"). The couple rely on their voices to guide themselves to each other and reunite with a kiss.

Variations/Tips
❑ Make the Bride and Groom use pet names for their better half. Or literally let them adopt the persona of their favorite pet and call to each other with barks, meows, or chirps, etc.
❑ If the couple is multilingual, they can call out "husband" and "wife" in another language.
❑ Increase the game's difficulty: have guests surround the perimeter of the square and do the calling. Male guests speak to the Bride, female guests speak to the Groom (limited to saying "oh darling") to help draw the couple into each other's arms.
❑ Include other couples, but blindfold only the men. Then situate the women about the square, they can call but can't move.
❑ Expand the game for an additional 10 couples. Stand the men in a line all facing one direction. Then the women randomly stand with their backs against the men's backs (the men and women can not see each other). Go to the first woman in the line (use a microphone if the gathering is large) and have her call out "Oh Darling!" Their partner replies "Here, sweetheart!" (they should feel free to adlib).

The two step to the head of the line. If the match is correct, the couple kiss and rejoin the audience. If the man is not her partner, both return to a different spot on the line and play resumes with the next woman.

PIN THE HOO-HA ON THE HE-MAN

Blindfolded players try to score a bulls-eye.

When
All girls bachelorette

How
Get a large sheet of paper, or tape newspaper together to form a large sheet. Draw an outline of a man that's about half life-sized. Affix the drawing to a wall. Make paper cut-outs of the male anatomy (it's funnier to vary the sizes a little) and put a little piece of tape on each studly member. Make enough cut-outs for all your players.

The Bride is the first one up. She gets blindfolded and must walk 5 paces to the drawing and affix the anatomy to the drawing. The first place she touches on the picture is where it goes--no feeling around! Every player takes turns. Whoever gets closest to the bulls-eye wins.

Variation/Tips
❑ Instead of recreated members, cut them out of a racy magazine, or give guests condoms to tack onto the proper place.

❑ Less risqué versions: enlarge a picture of the Groom, then have blindfolded players try to stick a plastic ring on his finger or a flower on his lapel.

❑ Spin blindfolded players two turns before turning them loose onto the drawing.

❑ Give each player a lip sticker and have her try to "kiss" the man on the cheek. (Write player's names on their stickers so a winner can be readily declared.) Or, have players put on an extra layer of lipstick on their lips and literally try to "kiss" the man on the lips.

Daily chores set the pace for this chair jockeying game.

When
Coed/all girls shower/bachelorette/reception

How
Any size group can play as long as there's a chair for each player and room to put all the chairs into a circle. One person stands in the circle's center as taskmaster, everybody else sits. Taskmaster loudly asks "Honey, did you <insert a household chore below> today?"

- brush your hair
- return a movie rental
- wash the car
- clean out the fridge
- make your bed
- gas up the car
- vacuum the home
- mow the lawn
- scrub the shower/tub
- clip your fingernails
- read e-mail
- tie your shoelaces
- read the newspaper
- take out the trash
- wash dishes
- walk the dog
- scrub the toilet bowl
- change a light bulb
- buy groceries
- brush your teeth
- make a phone call
- do laundry
- balance your checkbook
- eat breakfast
- bring in the mail
- mop the kitchen floor
- wash your hands
- iron clothes

All players answer at the same time. They say "yes" by moving to sit in the chair to their right or "no" by not moving... regardless of whether someone else is still in their seat. The next chore is called out, players answer by moving or staying seated, and so on.

The fun starts when a person moves to a chair still occupied by another (and sits on their lap)--you can get piles of slackers on one chair! It's very entertaining to see what daily activities people share in a day. Add chores to keep playing as desired.

Variation/Tips
❑ Let each player in the circle take turns calling out a unique chore.
❑ To include everyone at the reception, have all guests stand behind their chairs with a penny (each table is its own a circle). Players remain standing and move their penny from chair to chair.
❑ Number each chair, tell players to remember the chair they started in. First busy bee to return to their original seat wins.

SHELL SHOCKED

The Bride passes an egg through the Groom.

When
Coed bachelorette/reception

How
Give the Bride a hard-boiled egg (at room temperature) and instruct her to place the egg in one of the Groom's pant legs (with the Groom still in the pants of course) and guide it out the other pant leg. Sounds good, eh? It gets better. She's only allowed to use her mouth. No hands allowed!

If she can't handle this mouthful (she drops the egg or crushes it), she must perform a penalty.

Variation/Tips
❑ Egg them on by substituting a room temperature raw egg.

❑ Or, use a refrigerated hard-boiled egg or ping pong ball.

❑ Be a good egg by having the Groom stand on two chairs that have been placed side by side, one foot on each chair. This makes him more accessible for the Bride (who stands on the floor).

❑ To avoid egg on anyone's face, let the Bride use one hand only instead of her mouth--still plenty of racy fun.

❑ You can further tone down the egg-citment by having the Bride pass the egg from one end of the Groom's shirt sleeve (through the opening at the wrist) and out the other.

❑ If the couple are up for a real challenge, have them both pass a ping pong ball in their partner's shirt sleeve and out through the other sleeve at the same time with their hands. They race to see who can get their ball out first. It gets really funny when one player falls behind and cheats by hampering their partner's ball to catch up.

❑ Call up other couples to compete with the Bride and Groom.

SUCK FOR A BUCK

Daring men pay a dollar to suck it up--candy, that is.

When
All girls bachelorette

How
This game is perfect for a night of bar hopping with the Bride. Prepare a T-shirt the night before: write "Suck for a Buck" in permanent ink or iron-on letters across the front of a clean white tee.

Pin gummy candies or individually wrapped candies to her shirt. Or you can stick hard candies directly to the front of the shirt. If you choose to do this, slide a piece of wax paper in between the shirt to separate the front and back (this prevents the candy from seeping through). Dip one side of a small hard candy in a plate of very hot water briefly then apply that candy wet side down to the shirt. Apply at least 15 candies. Let the shirt dry overnight (use a fan to blow dry, if needed). Remove the paper and the T-shirt is ready.

Give the Bride-to-be her T-shirt to wear for your night out. Then, you and the gals take her out to a couple of bars. Men must pony up a buck to suck or nibble a piece of candy off her shirt. If guys are shy, have attendees sweet talk some sugar daddies over.

Variation/Tips
❑ A tamer alternative: bachelorette carries a basket of suckers or bubble gum to sell for a buck. Tamer still: write "Kiss for a Buck" on the shirt, then have the bachelorette sell chocolate Kisses®.

❑ The brave can try "Hooters for Dollars." Purchase a pair of blow-up or rubber breasts from a costume shop and strap 'em on the outside of the bachelorette's bra (but under her shirt). Any guy who gives her a dollar gets a flash of her silicone hooters.

❑ Use the money to reimburse the cost of the game and give the balance to the Bride; or let the gang split the loot.

THE SWEETEST KISS

The Groom fishes for sweets in his Bride's mouth.

When
Coed bachelorette/reception

How
Give three different flavors of hard candies (such as Lifesavers®) to the Bride to place in her mouth. Tell the Groom his job is to remove the candy by going mouth to mouth--no hands. Not only that, the Groom must retrieve each flavor in a specific order.

Solicit the audience for the flavor priority (cherry first, coconut second, etc.). The Groom must do their bidding, otherwise he performs a penalty for each incorrect flavor he draws. Refer to the Appendix for penalty ideas.

Variation/Tips
❑ Turn the tables by making it the Bride's responsibility to retrieve each flavor from the Groom's mouth.

❑ This game can be expanded to include couples in a Jack and Jill party.

TO HAVE AND TO HOLD

Test a couple's ability to plant kisses on their amore.

When
Coed shower/reception

How
You'll need three bags worth of chocolate Kisses® to play. Call up two couples to compete against the Bride and Groom, this makes three separate teams. The men can stand in any position they want, long as they're set in a row, facing the audience, at least an arm width apart from one another.

Give each woman a bag of chocolate. The gals have to balance as many kisses as they can on their partner's body (arms, head, feet, etc.). The pair that comes up with a way to plant the most kisses within one minute wins. Any kisses that fall off don't count.

Variation/Tips
- ❑ Substitute heart shaped candy for chocolate, if desired.
- ❑ You may want to set a ground rule that they can't pour chocolate into their partner's clothes or pockets. Other hints you might want to provide: players may squat to create more surface area (the legs) or get on their hands and knees (to use their entire back) for collecting kisses. No lying down allowed!
- ❑ A simpler variation: pour all the chocolates into a bucket. Have each woman grab as many kisses as she can with both hands on one try. Now their male partners guess how many kisses his counterpart is holding. The women compete among themselves to see who can grab the most chocolate, the men compete to see who can come closest to guessing the actual number of sweets grabbed by their partner. Once the guesses are in, have couples count the chocolates grabbed by the team to their right (so nobody is counting their own kisses). Split the chocolates between the male and female winner.

UP TO SNUFF

See if the Bride can follow her Groom's nose.

When
Coed shower/bachelorette/reception

How
To play, you'll need a large opaque cloth (about 8' X 8'). Cut a small hole in the center about 5' up from the bottom edge, the hole should be big enough for a nose to fit through. Ask two volunteers to stand on chairs and hold the cloth up during the game.

Select five couples, such as the Bride and bridesmaids and their partners. Line the men up behind the cloth so that the women can't see them. Each man takes a turn putting their nose through the hole. The ladies try to identify the man behind the nostril. Write down their guesses. Ask the next man to hold his nose in the air for scrutiny, and continue until all the men have had their turn to nose around.

Ask man number one to reveal himself and give a point to each correct answer. Continue with the reveals. The woman who hits it on the nose with the most correct answers is your winner.

Variation/Tips

❏ Have each man behind the cloth go to the back of the line after their turn, that way they're in the correct order for the reveal.

❏ Keep the women at least three feet away from the cloth or they may be able to see through the hole and cheat.

❏ Instead of asking each woman in turn, ask them to just pipe up if she thinks she recognizes her partner's olfactory appendage. If more than one gal lays claim to a nosepiece, all the funnier.

❏ Put the Bride on the spot by making just her guess the identity of each man. Then reveal them after she's made her guesses.

❏ Cut 5 small holes in the cloth, have all 5 men put their noses through. Ask the Bride to sniff out her Groom and the Maid of Honor to nose in on the Best Man. Then drop the cloth.

❏ Let the Groom put his nose to the grindstone with this variation. Ask the Bride and a number of women to put on lipstick and kiss a white piece of paper. Have the Groom guess which imprint came from his wife's lips.

WEDDING PORTRAITS

Pose for a picture worth a thousand laughs.

When
Coed shower/bachelorette/reception

How
You'll need a second room to briefly hold players, they should not be able to hear what's going on in the main room during the game.

Ask four guys and four gals to volunteer to play. This is funnier when the guys and gals don't know one another and are of various ages. Stand them in a line, alternating boy-girl-boy. Select the first three players in line and send the rest to the holding room.

The first two players represent the Groom and Bride. The third player is a wedding photographer who gets to pose the mock couple into the funniest wedding picture he can create. When the mischievous shutter bug is finished, observers should applaud the poser's efforts. Now, surprise the photog with this news: he must take the place of the guy in his portrait!

The man relieved from the still life retrieves the next player in line, a woman. She too is told to arrange the new pair into a silly photo. After she is done, she must take the place of the female in her tableaux. Game continues until the rest of the players have had their turn.

Variations/Tips
❑ Warn players and audience members not to give the secret away before bringing in a new player.

❑ The emcee may want to enforce ground rules to prevent players from being posed in ways that make everyone uncomfortable. On the other hand, the emcee may want to encourage and suggest creative, funny poses to a timid photographer.

❑ To juice this up for a bachelorette, tell photographers to arrange their subjects into romantic poses.

❑ If you're in a small venue and there is no second waiting room available, send the players outside.

WHERE'S HUNTLEY?

The engaged spends her night on the town collecting
bachelor autographs.

When
Coed/all girls bachelorette

How
This game is most effectively played while bar or club hopping.

Prepare a T-shirt by clearly handwriting 20 to 30 names of common
and not so common men's names on the front and back of the shirt:
David, Peter, Omar, Greg, Ian, Matt, Steve, Martin, Huntley, etc.

The Bride-to-be wears the shirt on the evening out and should ask
every Tom, Dick, and Harry for his name. If his name is on her shirt,
he has to sign her shirt as proof. Tell the Bride she will have to
perform a penalty for each unclaimed name at the end of the evening.

Variations/Tips
❑   Wear a second shirt underneath the first to prevent ink from
    accidentally seeping through onto the skin.
❑   Write only guy names that begin with letters from the Bride's
    name.
❑   If you prefer positive motivation, do away with the penalty and
    give the Bride a dollar for each name she can get autographed.

FUN ACTIVITIES

ADDRESS AN ENVELOPE

Lottery to get thank you envelopes accurately addressed.

When
Coed/all girls shower/reception

How
Give to each person attending a 2"x4" white self-adhesive label, ask them to neatly print their name and address on the label for a drawing. Collect the labels. Draw a winner and award a small prize.

The "real" prize is for the Bride who now has all her guests' up-to-date addresses to apply to the envelopes of her thank you notes.

Variation/Tips
❏ Use this contest to draw names to giveaway table centerpieces to lucky guests who might otherwise fight over them.
❏ Instead of asking guests to sign and address a guest book, ask them to add a leaf to the "tree of love." Cut out a variety of hearts, run an ornament hook (or ribbon) through each one. Guests each take a heart and print a brief congratulatory note on one side, their name and address on the other. Provide a small tree for guests to hang the hearts on. (The tree can be an artificial plant or a dried tree branch.) Randomly draw a heart to award a prize, if desired. If guests aren't particularly wordy people, ask them to print a single adjective (like vivacious, thrilled, blissful, etc.) describing the couple.
❏ For a more personalized variation of the above variation, ask guests to trace their hands on a piece of cardstock or construction paper. They cut out their handprint, write their message, and hang up their greetings.

CALL FOR A KISS

Celebrants clink their glasses to demand lip service.

When
Reception

How
Anytime guests are seated, pick up a fork and "clink" it repeatedly against your glass. Most people know about this tradition to quickly join in. Don't stop the racket until the Bride and Groom agree to stand and kiss for the crowd.

This is very entertaining when the couple is shy about public displays of affection. Peruse the variations below to liven up this game for jaded players.

Variation/Tips
❑ The couple requires a guest at the clinking table (or the entire table) to perform a stunt or dare before conceding to press lips. The stunt might be along the lines of singing a portion of a song that contains the word "love" or doing push-ups or see penalties in the Appendix for more ideas. Write these stunts on individual pieces of paper and tuck into balloons for people to pop to get their assignment.

❑ Ask guests to show off a special talent of theirs to earn the kiss.

❑ Place a picture of a farmyard animal (cow, pig, chicken, goat, duck, etc.) at each table. Whenever a table clinks, they stand and do their best rendition of that animal to see the love peck.

❑ The newlyweds select two unlikely guests at the clinking table to demonstrate how the couple should kiss, Bride & Groom must duplicate the demonstrated exchange. Tables will be only too excited to bang their glasses to witness lip wrestling between a young stud and grandma. If it's mostly established couples attending who would be reluctant to peck someone else, have couples themselves demonstrate the lip lock. If the Bride and Groom want to keep control over how they'll be made to smooch, establish this ground rule: simply tell your guests that the price for a newlywed kiss is a kiss between any couple.

❑ Guests fold paper airplanes to fly across a room and land in a specific spot (or box) to initiate a kissing call.

❑ Guests have to give some sentimental or silly marital advice to initiate the bridal smooch.

❑ A table must correctly answer a trivia question about the couple (see the Appendix for ideas) to induce marital face pressing.

- A couple must re-enact their own wedding proposal. Or, a couple roasts the honorees with a dramatization of how the newlyweds "really" wanted to propose to each other.
- Give everyone bells to ring their request for lip service.
- Set up a ring toss or other carnival type tossing game so for each successful toss a guest makes, the newlyweds kiss. To up the ante, tell any guest who tries but fails that the newlyweds get to select someone who the attempting guest has to kiss.
- See Olympic Kissing in the Pranks chapter.

MARRIAGE IS...

Present a humorous collection of wedlock wisdom to the Bride and Groom.

When
Reception

How
With a pad and paper, ask children and men to complete the following sentence, "Marriage is…." and write down their answers.

After you've collected enough to pick and choose from, take a sheet of parchment paper and print in bold letters "Marriage is…" at the top of the page, then neatly write the funniest fill-ins (and attribute the name of the sage behind the insight) on the parchment.

Roll it up, tie with a ribbon and present to the newlyweds.

Variation/Tips
- Have the best man and maid of honor take turns reading a few of the cuter answers to the reception for entertainment. This gives the Bride and Groom a chance to eat/rest.

PANTRY INTRODUCTIONS

Sarah brings sugar, June arrives with jam, Caitlin enters with coffee...

When
Coed/all girls shower

How
Instruct attendees in the shower invitation to bring a food item that begins with the same letter as their first name and that uniqueness will be rewarded. For example, Tiffany could bring anything from tomato sauce to tortillas to tea.

Early in the shower, ask each guest to introduce him or herself to the group and then present the Bride with the grocery item to help stock her pantry.

The Bride awards a small prize to the one who made the most innovative use of the first letter of their first name.

Variation/Tips
❑ Get more mileage out of this game by requesting that everybody bring an item that comes in a can only. Then after everybody has made their introductions and presented the cans in a pile, ask trivia questions of the Bride regarding the Groom (and vice versa if he's playing too). For each question she answers wrong, tear off the label from a can before giving the can to the Bride. Correct answers are rewarded with a can that still has its label intact.

❑ A different idea is to instruct guests to bring a gift for the couple that the giver cannot live without (or is a timesaver). Invitees introduce themselves before the group and explain why their particular gadget is so important to them that they can't live without it.

RANDOM WINNER

The lucky guest who catches a star wins the coveted
table centerpiece.

When
Reception

How
Randomly attach a star sticker under one plate from each table before
the guests arrive. During the gathering, before the dishes get cleared,
announce the table centerpieces will be awarded as random prizes.
Tell everyone to look underneath their plate for the star. If they have
the star, they may claim the centerpiece as their prize.

Variation/Tips
- ❑ Stick a star underneath chairs instead of plates.
- ❑ Make the winner perform a stunt or dare before awarding them the
  centerpiece. See penalties in the Appendix for ideas.
- ❑ This can also be used as a way to draft players for group games
  and ensures that each table has one representative.
- ❑ Have guests pass a napkin around their table as music plays.
  When the music stops, the person with the napkin waves it in the
  air for all to see. Then, tell them to give the napkin to the person
  on their left--this is the person who actually gets the centerpiece.
- ❑ Another variation of the above variation: get a person at each
  table to volunteer a dollar to pass, just like the napkin. Once music
  stops, tell the person who's holding the dollar he's won--the right
  to give the centerpiece to the person who volunteered the dollar.
- ❑ Create a scavenger-type hunt among participants. Whoever
  produces the requested article first wins the centerpiece. Some
  possible items to ask for: a picture of their mother-in-law, a coin
  from the same year as the Bride/Groom's birth year, condoms, a
  feather, aspirin, a golf ball, etc.
- ❑ Mark as many pennies as you have centerpieces with removable
  tape. Hide the pennies around the venue... try tucking one in the
  centerpiece, under a plate, next to the stage, or scattered around
  the floor. Guests have to find the penny to win a centerpiece.
  Provide hints if players are having a difficult time.
- ❑ Mark off a grid of 5 by 5 squares on the floor with masking tape.
  Use tape to mark each square with a unique number. Prepare
  scraps with numbers that match the grid. Played like Musical
  Chairs, players must find a square to stand on when the music
  stops. Pull a number, whoever is on that number wins a prize.
- ❑ Award centerpieces as prizes for any other games in this book.

Fresh ways to get the bouquet and garter out to the singles.

When
Reception

How
Call all the single men to the dance floor. They form a circle, but face out. The Bride and Groom stand in the center of the men's circle. Now call all the single women to form a circle around the men, facing in (the men and women now face each other).

The newly wedded husband removes the garter from his wife's leg. She then takes the garter and gives it to one of the women in the circle. He gives the bouquet to one of the men.

Start playing music, saying this is a race to see which circle can pass their item the fastest. The women quickly pass the garter within their circle and men pass the bouquet within theirs. Let the goods make a round or two, then suddenly stop the music. Reveal the true purpose of this activity: whoever's stuck holding the garter and bouquet are the ones who have "caught" the wedding giveaways.

Variation/Tips
❑ To take this farther, have the man give his bouquet to the woman and she slide the garter up his leg for keeps.
❑ Or, have the men surround the women with chairs so the ladies can play musical chairs. Eliminate two chairs each round (this means two men and two women are cut), until there's only one man and woman left. At the start of the game, give each man a number, randomly draw numbers to determine which men get cut.
❑ For career-minded men or women reluctant to catch the garter or bouquet because of its traditional meaning, tell the bachelors that whoever catches the toss wins an award or privilege. Depending on what motivates the bachelors, it might be their first pick of a dance partner or exchanging a kiss with the person who caught the other item. Or, the garter and bouquet catcher get the honor of picking a pair of guests to create an amusingly mismatched couple to demonstrate how to kiss for the Bride and Groom (see Call for a Kiss variations).
❑ Attach cool cash to the garter/bouquet for more enthusiasm.
❑ Invite everybody--married and single--to try to catch the bouquet/garter. Tell them that in this case, catching it means catching some good luck.

- Give more opportunities to grab destiny: prepare a bouquet composed of a cluster of mini-bouquets with fortunes tied to each bunch. Write warm fortunes that predict the catcher's love connection: "You'll marry your true love.", "He will be your best friend." and "Your future husband is waiting for you." etc. When the time comes, fling the whole cluster at once so that it comes apart as it falls.
- An informal way to distribute the bouquet is to take it apart and personally hand each flower to an unattached individual.
- Make a real competition out of the toss. Set a large, open cardboard box in the middle of the dance floor, stand single ladies in a line about five feet away, their backs to the box. Give each woman a penny taped to a tissue (write a unique number on each). At the word "Go," they simultaneously toss their tissue over their head, whoever lands their tissue in the box wins the bouquet. If you have a tie, hold a tiebreaker with the box farther away.
- Toss out the toss altogether, have a duplicate Bride's bouquet made. Present each to the Bride's and Groom's mother as a gift.

VIP CONGRATULATIONS

The President of the United States sends his congratulations to the wedding couple.

When
Reception

How
At least six weeks before the wedding, send a wedding invitation to the man in the oval office at The White House, Attn: Greetings Office, Washington, DC 20502-0039. Include a stamp, your address, and phone number. Request the reply be sent to your attention so you can surprise the engaged. His staff will try to reply 10 days prior to the event with well wishes from the President.

Variation/Tips
- If unable to send a wedding invitation, provide the couple's names, wedding date, as well as your phone number and address.
- Take note, the White House also sends greetings for couples celebrating their 50th anniversary or better, and baby births.
- Write on the couple's behalf to their favorite celebrity or hometown mayor requesting a note of congratulations.
- Catholic couples may request a blessing from the Pope: Prefettura della Casa Pontifica, 00120 Citta del Vaticano, Italia.

PRANKS

BALLOONS

Gas the newlywed's car with helium-filled condoms.

When
After the reception/morning after wedding

How
Purchase an economy sized box of non-lubricated condoms and a tank of helium. Blow up 30 condom balloons and tie them off tightly at the ends with ribbon. Sneak the balloons into their car so that the bouquet is ready to greet the newlyweds when they come for their car.

Variation/Tips
- ❑ Create variety by purchasing textured, ribbed, and colored condoms as well as plain.
- ❑ If helium isn't readily available, gather a couple of strong lungs to inflate your special balloons the old fashioned way.
- ❑ Tie a balloon on their car antenna.
- ❑ Decorate their honeymoon suite with these phallic balloons.
- ❑ Let your imagination go wild and pump unusual items with helium to create a lighter than air world: latex gloves, floating pool toys such as a swimmer's ring, other inflatable decorations found in a party supply store.

THE BETA SPEECH

When there's trouble accessing a speech written on a memory stick, the speaker reverts to the beta version.

When
Reception

How
Your speaker stands with the microphone, announces he/she has a few words to say about the Bride and Groom. The speaker pulls a computer memory stick out of his pocket, asks if there's a computer handy. Of course there isn't, so he shrugs and declares, "Looks like I have to go to the beta version." And pulls out the actual speech on index cards.

Variation/Tips
❑ If you don't have a memory stick handy, any CD works as well.

❑ A tech savvy audience may give a bigger laugh if you start reading a written speech filled with bad jokes and puns, stop and comment, "This speech is awful, isn't it?" pretend to take a closer look at the speech and remark, "No wonder, it's the beta version." and pull out the polished/actual speech. (In tech terminology, the beta version is usually an early release used for testing to fine-tune what will be the finished product.)

❑ After someone has finished a lengthy speech, have the videographer step in and say the batteries on his camera died during the speech and could the speaker please repeat the speech.

❑ During the reception, discretely pass out actual pieces of toasted bread slices to your guests. Tell them to wait for your signal. Take the stage and loudly ask if anybody would like to toast the Bride and Groom. This is the cue for all guests to toss their toasts at the couple.

BRAVEST OF THEM ALL

Dare the Groom to show the most bravado in egg roulette.

When
Reception

How
During the reception, summon the groomsmen and Groom before the crowd on the dance floor. Praise the men for their close friendship. Declare that life is full of uncertainty, so this game will test their nerves.

Hold up a collection of eggs (one for each player). Explain that all but one of the eggs is hard boiled. They are each to take turns selecting an egg and smashing it against their forehead.

Obviously, the unlucky individual who selects the sole fresh egg will get quite messy. What you keep secret from the players is that *every* egg is hardboiled. Make the Groom go last. Enjoy watching each man squirm, especially the Groom, as he works up the courage to smash his egg.

Variation/Tips
❑ You can tell all the groomsmen (but not the Groom) beforehand that all the eggs are hardboiled so they can ham up their acts of fearlessness. After you've made the Groom sweat a while, a groomsman can make a show of sacrificing himself for his buddy by offering to smash the final egg on himself. Get the Groom to owe him big time before revealing the joke's on him.

❑ This works even better if the Maid of Honor (or Bride herself) is behind this prank, what Groom would turn down a dare from his beloved's best friend?

❑ If the Groom's entourage is small, or there's just one best man, pull up a few brave-hearts from those attending the reception to participate.

A congratulatory handshake is a chance to palm a surprise to the Groom.

When
Reception

How
During the reception, discreetly pass out condoms to participating pranksters. Have them hide it in the palm of their hand so that when they shake with the Groom, he'll receive the condom. If the jokesters are subtle, the gag will only be known to the Groom who is busy stuffing his pockets.

Variation/Tips
❑ To carry this gag out further, stuff condoms in the couple's car, like in the sun visor, glove compartment, into the seat cushions, and in the side pockets.
❑ Check out the Balloons prank if you have extra condoms.

COVER UP

The bachelorette must charm men out of their pants to clothe her special friend.

When
Coed/all girl's bachelorette

How
Not for the faint-hearted! Play this game in conjunction with an evening out on the town. When you're ready to go out, use yarn to tie the bachelorette's wrist to the wrist of a naked blow-up doll. She has by the end of the event to dress her air-head companion. But, she can only use clothes donated to her by chivalrous men encountered in the evening.

If the Bride-to-be fails to cajole enough clothing off of stranger's backs (Mr. Happy would really look cuter with a hat, don't you think?), she must perform a penalty.

Variation/Tips
❏ Some establishments may not grant admittance to a blow-up doll. Research this ahead of time to avoid disappointment. If this is a problem, play a coed version "in house" or start the doll off with undies.

THE FIRST DANCE

The Groom interrupts the father and daughter dance for hilarity.

When
Reception

How
As the Bride and her father are finishing up their first dance, the Groom breaks in. Instead of dancing with his wife, the Groom sweeps his father-in-law off his feet.

Variation/Tips
❑ Let the father-in-law in on the prank ahead of time so that it goes smoothly.

❑ An alternative: sometime while the Bride is dancing with her Groom, have the Groom's best man step up to request a dance and boogie off with the Groom in tow.

GARTER UP

Sliding a garter up a woman's leg gets a whole lot hairier.

When
Reception

How
Have the single woman who caught the bouquet take a seat. Instruct the man who caught the garter to kneel in front of the woman. Explain that he has to slide the garter up the woman's leg using only his teeth. Tell him that for modesty's sake, he will have to be blindfolded.

After he is blindfolded, quickly switch the woman with the Groom and see how far your bachelor gets before he wises up.

Variation/Tips
❑ Or, have Groom wear a garter under his pants and have the Bride make a big show of reaching into the Groom's leg for the garter.

116

Players wearing paper sacks over their heads fail to realize victory is in the bag.

When
Coed/all girls bachelorette/shower

How
The host calls for between 3 and 6 volunteers to play a "special" game. Only the fastest and smartest players need apply.

Hand each player a paper bag and tell them to put it over their heads. The object of the "game" is to take off anything they're wearing that's not necessary. The person with the biggest pile of discards wins. Most people take off their shoes, jacket, watch, etc. It takes a while, if ever, for them to remember the bag. Meanwhile, those sitting it out get to enjoy the player's puzzlement.

Variation/Tips
❏ To prevent a smarty-pants player from asking if they can remove the bag and thus tip off the other players, tell them beforehand that once the game starts, there's no questions allowed until the game is over.

❏ Give a time limit of two minutes to create a sense of urgency.

HELP ME

A message appears when the Groom kneels at the altar.

When
Wedding

How
Use strips of masking tape to write "help" on the bottom of the Groom's left shoe and "me" on the Groom's right shoe. The letters should be oriented so that the back of the heel borders the top of the message.

Variation/Tips
❑ Extra consideration should be applied to this practical joke. If this will more likely offend guests than crack them up, skip it!

❑ Another message to try: sold.

❑ Couldn't get to the shoes in time? Sprinkle baby powder at the location where the Groom is expected to kneel.

HEN PARTY

The Groom organizes an unusual girl's night out for his Bride.

When
All girls bachelorette

How
The Groom tells his Bride to let him plan a girl's night out for her, implying that it's going to be a bachelorette party. He should talk it up, telling her how much fun she'll have. Then invite the mothers-in-law, grandmas, aunts, and any women she's not very close with to the restaurant. Blindfold the Bride and escort her in. She'll be surprised by the choice in attendees.

Halfway through dinner, the Groom declares that he has a terrible headache and asks his intended to step out for some fresh air with him. The Groom drives her to another location and takes her to a room that, surprise, is filled with her closest friends. The let-down-your-hair party she originally expected begins.

Variation/Tips
❑ Tactfully inform the first group of invitees beforehand that you plan to kidnap the guest of honor during the dinner for a "romantic surprise" and that they need to keep this a secret. Ditto for the second group.

❑ Brides can pull a similar stunt on their Grooms. Tell him you're planning a night of debauchery involving many beautiful women for him. Then bring him blindfolded to a dinner with mothers-in-law, grandmas, aunts, etc. Have cameras ready when you let "the girls" playfully caress their greetings to your man, then yank off the blindfold.

Laughable reasons for bravely speaking up now instead of forever holding your peace.

When
Wedding

How
Discuss and plan this prank with the minister or officiant. Prepare 10 pieces of letter sized cardstock with a drawing of the international symbol for peace on both sides.

At the gathering, discreetly distribute the cards to a bunch of people sitting toward the front. When the official says "...or forever hold your peace." Have everyone hold up their "peace."

Variation/Tips
❏ Make sure the couple has the same sense of humor as you do and wouldn't be offended by this kind of interruption.
❏ When the appropriate moment in the ceremony arrives, have a young boy run down the aisle calling the Groom, "Daddy! Daddy!"
❏ A bolder variation is to have a man burst in and declare that he's in love with the Bride while trashing the Groom. The actor should make his tirade as he marches up the aisle. When he gets close enough to the couple, he stares at them a moment and says, "Whoops! Wrong wedding!" then runs out of the ceremony.

THE INCREDIBLE TEDDY

The last gift to the Bride is a racy teddy so wild that it has to be seen to be believed.

When
Coed/all girls bachelorette/shower

How
After the last gift is opened at the party, announce that you saved the best for last. Hold up a large bag from a women's lingerie store (or department store) and tell the Bride-to-be that the bag holds the most wild and exotic teddy ever. Embellish wildly.

Ask for a volunteer to model the teddy to the engaged. Randomly pick a woman. Send her to the bathroom with the bag. Inside the gift bag is a large stuffed teddy bear, a bath towel, and a note you've prepared: "I need your help with this prank. Please act as if you've just seen the most unbelievable piece of lingerie and peek out the restroom declaring how shocked and embarrassed you are. Say that you can't wear this, then agree to let me help you. Thanks!"

When the volunteer refuses to wear the teddy, pretend to cajole her, then rush into the bathroom to "help." Roll up the model's pant legs and sleeves so that it looks as if she's not wearing any clothes once the bath towel is wrapped around her. Have her hold the teddy bear in front of her, then wrap the towel around them both so that her bare arms and legs are showing.

Lead her back to the group. Announce to the gathering, "OK, I hope nobody here has a weak heart. Here is the incredible teddy!" and drop the towel.

Variation/Tips
❑   This joke is more convincing if you pick a volunteer you've never met before. Try to recruit an outgoing personality.
❑   Deter spoilsports who insist you do the modeling by whispering this excuse: a bad skin rash that just started today.
❑   Dress the teddy bear in lingerie intended for the engaged.

The newlyweds retire to their hotel room and discover a room full of gags.

When
After the wedding

How
The morning of the wedding, get the key to their hotel room using any excuse that doesn't raise suspicion, such as "I'll drop off your luggage in your room for you." or "Let me hold onto your keys so you don't have to worry about losing them."

Pepper the room with imaginative pranks. Fill their tub with shaving cream. Wrap the toilet bowl tightly with plastic wrap (underneath the seat and lid) so that the wrap is not easily visible. Substitute bed sheets that are too short for the bed (or take them away entirely, leaving only the cover). Attach a bunch of bells or squeak toys to the bed. Hide a bunch of cheap alarm clocks all around to the room and set them to go off at random times. Empty the Bride and Groom's luggage leaving them something silly like a g-string and pasties. Hide a blow-up doll in the closet.

After letting the couple squirm for a little bit, invite them to the room you've booked next door where nothing has been tampered with and let them enjoy their privacy.

Variation/Tips
❑ This elaborate stunt requires planning and is easier to pull off with the help of an additional friend.
❑ Do not do any permanent damage to the room, the hotel will charge you for it. Make sure you clean up the room and return anything you removed before checking out!
❑ After sending the newlyweds off to their real honeymoon room, use the prank room to host an after-party.

JEEPERS PEEPERS

Trick women into thinking they gave a peeping tom an eyeful.

When
Coed bachelorette

How
Select three women who are wearing skirts or dresses. Place two eggs, about one foot apart, on the ground. Tell the women the goal is to be able to step over the eggs without crushing them while blindfolded. Blindfold all three, lead them one at a time near the eggs and let them think they've successfully stepped over the eggs. After all three are done, have a man from the group quickly lie down so that his head is where the eggs originally were.

Tell the gals to remove their blindfolds. See who is most embarrassed at the thought of giving a total stranger an eyeful. After everybody has had their laugh, offer a gift to the reddest face and let them in on what really happened.

Variation/Tips
❑ Record the gag from start to finish on video (or with a camera) to provide reassurance to disbelieving prank victims.

JOINED AT THE HEAD

The Bride and maid of honor are so close they have the ability to read the other's mind.

When
Coed/all girls bachelorette/shower/reception

How
You, the maid of honor, announce to the audience how close you and the Bride are. In fact, you're such good and close friends that you two can literally read each other's minds. To prove it, you have the Bride leave the room and ask random members of the audience to pick any 5 items in the room (it could be a man's wallet, a woman's necklace, a bottle of champagne, anything). You brag that the Bride will return to the room and be able to tell what they picked by reading your mind.

When the Bride returns, you travel the room while pointing to different objects and asking, "Is it this table?" She shakes her head. "Is it his watch?" and the Bride might say, "Oh heavens no!", "Is it her scarf?" Another negative. And you ask, "Is it his wallet?" to which the Bride suddenly shouts "Yes!" and she would be right.

How did you two do it? You have prearranged a signal. You point to something black right before pointing to the correct object! Have fun dazzling your guests.

Variation/Tips
❑ Practice this bit beforehand so that it looks totally convincing. The Bride can make a big show of trying to read the maid of honor's mind by rubbing her forehead and making comments like, "Work with me here!" or "Think louder."

NEAT GOWNS

Neatness counts, but not where they expected.

When
Coed/all girls bachelorette/shower

How
Give each guest a tightly sealed business-sized envelope with a folded piece of 8.5"x11" white paper inside it. Guests write their name on the front of their envelope. Send the Bride out of the room.

Tell guests they have one minute to open their envelope and construct the prettiest gown they can out of their one sheet of paper (with no tape or scissors). When time is up, everyone returns their envelope and hangs onto their gowns. Bring the Bride back in. Now, reveal the true object of the game: the Bride will award a prize to the person who opened their envelope the neatest!

Variation/Tips
❑ To add a second part to the game, collect all the gowns with the envelopes before the Bride's return. After the Bride judges the neatest envelope, let her try to identify which gown belongs to which guest.

❑ Ask players to autograph their designer dresses, then collect the gowns for the scrapbook.

OLYMPIC KISSING

The newlyweds kiss and score.

When
Reception

How
Prepare 8 to 10 sheets of 8.5" x 11" white cardstock. With a black marker, write a score on each sheet ranging from −3 to 10. Quietly pass out score cards to the groomsmen and bridesmaids at the reception. Flash the cards when the happy couple kiss.

Variation/Tips
❑ Plan in advance so that everybody knows to show their cards at a prearranged signal, like when the newlyweds exchange their first peck after a round of glass clinking (see Call for A Kiss).

❑ Write the numbers thickly so they can be seen from a distance.

Transform the happy couple's car into a rolling pronouncement of their recent union.

When
Before/after wedding/reception

How
Look in a well-stocked craft store for temporary window markers or window "chalk" in a pen designed for writing messages on windows. Write messages only on the side windows to prevent obstructing the driver's front and rear views. Have someone distract the Bride and Groom while you work.

Traditional favorite phrases: Just married!, John loves Jane, Tied the knot, Always and Forever, Together at last, I married my best friend, Kiss the Bride, Happily ever after, and Congratulations.

More creative slogans: To bed or bust!, Honey bunnies, Off the market for good, Finally!, Honk if you're in love, Staying in tonight, Yay!, S/he finally got him/her, Internet lovers, Newlyweds on board, or True love rules!

Variation/Tips
❑ Do NOT apply anything that might damage the car's paint.
❑ Affix fake flowers, plastic pom-poms, curled ribbon, tulle, and/or bows to the outside of the car.
❑ Swath the car's exterior/interior in toilet paper or white tulle.
❑ Tuck rice into both sun visors so that there's one last hurrah when the visors are pulled down.
❑ Tie a naughty novelty toy to the car's rear view mirror or antenna.
❑ See the Balloons prank for additional ideas.

Air-heads greet the newlyweds at home.

When
After the wedding

How
You'll need access to the newlywed's home while they are out of the house for a couple of hours minimum.

Purchase several, or as many as your wallet can handle, cheap blow-up dolls. You'll also need several spray cans of insulation foam (it's a special kind of foam that hardens in a few minutes) from a hardware store.

First, loosely blow up a doll to create space inside for the foam filling. You may need to cut a small hole in the back of the doll in order to fill it with insulation foam. Before the foam completely hardens, position the doll in funny poses throughout the home: sitting on the toilet, bent over the bed, swinging from the chandelier, etc.

Variation/Tips
❑ Instead of filling the blow-up dolls with foam, try helium for a unique gift bouquet.

STRIP TEASER

A masked male stripper with a very familiar ring about him.

When
All girls bachelorette

How
Ask the Groom to put on a strip show for his Bride, but have him don an elaborate mask and costume cause she won't be told it's him.

During the party, tell the Bride you've hired a male stripper for her and bring him in. He should have a boom box with him to play a heart-thumping song. The Groom should get real physical with her, like taking her hands and placing it on his undulating waist and points south. If the Bride hasn't figured it out by the time he's down to his undies, rip off the mask.

Variation/Tips
❑ If you think the Bride can easily recognize her hubby-to-be, blindfold the Bride during the strip show and have the Groom/stripper flirt like crazy with her body. Then, when the Bride is blushing enough, remove her blindfold so that she can see who her amazing stripper was.

❑ Hire a real stripper for the Bride, but arrange to have the Groom crash the party and pretend to throw a jealousy fit.

SUBTITLED SPEECH

A wedding speech that suffers from bad subtitling.

When

Coed shower/reception

How

On several sheets of white foam board, write up a speech in another language (perhaps the Bride or Groom's secondary language, if applicable) or plain English. When the appropriate speech is begun by the speaker, hold up the subtitles for the audience, running them upside down and out of sequence!

Variation/Tips

❑ Let the original speech writer in on the joke so that you can work together to write up the subtitled speech.

❑ For increased comedic effect, write the subtitles in a variety of languages or a language that no one at the gathering speaks or reads. The internet has a lot of free translation programs that you can use to translate the speech into another language.

RETURN OF THE KEYS

An overwhelming return of the Bride's extra house keys.

When
Reception

How
Quietly pass out single keys to 10 to 20 men in the reception (mainly guests, an elderly gentleman, maybe a waiter at the restaurant, etc.).

Set a bowl in front of the Bride and announce: "Now that Jane is married, will those who had a copy of her apartment key please turn them in?" Your key men should line up to "return" their key to the Bride.

Variation/Tips
❑ Try this gag on the Groom, just pass out keys to lots of women.
❑ If doing the return of keys for both the Bride and Groom, have the Bride get a lot of returns, and the Groom get a return from a guy and an older woman only, or vice versa.

THE SHORT OF IT

Watch mayhem ensue when the wedding party discovers their shoes have spontaneously shrunk.

When
Day of wedding

How
Purchase a duplicate pair of the Bride or Groom's wedding day shoes that's two sizes smaller than the original. On the morning of the wedding, switch the correctly sized shoes with the smaller ones and have a camera rolling as they get dressed for the wedding.

Variation/Tips
❑ Instead of shoes, switch the Groom's jacket.
❑ Make the shoes/jacket two sizes bigger, not smaller.

WRONG SHOWER

A talkative guest thinks there's a bun in the Bride's oven.

When
Coed/all girls shower

How
Solicit the help of a mischievous gal that the Bride and her friends do not know. Create a fake baby shower invitation for a house near the actual bridal shower. Instruct your accomplice, the Stranger, to come to the shower 30 minutes late and bring a large purse with baby gifts and the baby shower invitation stuffed at the bottom.

Once she arrives, she quietly mingles. Let the sharp-eyed Bride-to-be confront the Stranger directly. The Stranger offers her hearty congratulations, "reminds" her they're co-workers (prep her with some information), and remarks how much she glows, asks if she's feeling nauseous yet, has she picked a name, etc.

You run up and ask to see the Stranger's invitation. The Stranger then digs through her purse, pulling out baby bottles, rattles, diapers, crackers, etc. with bows stuck on them. When she produces the invitation, point out she's at the wrong address. That this is a bridal, not baby, shower and guide her out. After a minute, bring the Stranger back and introduce her as your prankster in crime.

Variation/Tips
❑ Do not attempt this joke if the Bride is unreceptive toward sharing the spotlight or detours from planned activities.

❑ Tell your victims they're to try to recall and write down everything they can remember in the Stranger's purse.

❑ A simpler version: give an attendee a prepared purse with unusual items (flask, stuffed animal, highlighter pen, etc.). When everyone is seated, the attendee suddenly spills her purse onto the floor. After everyone has helped her put everything back, announce the game is to recall all the items they just saw. Make a competition out of it by passing out pen and paper, player who remembers the most items wins.

APPENDIX

TRIVIA QUESTIONS

These questions supplement certain games within this book. Feel free to add to this list. Other uses for trivia: Place a list of five questions on each reception table to entertain guests. Challenge the Bride's family with questions about the Groom and his family about the Bride. Some cultures have a wedding day tradition of quizzing the Groom, making him earn his way into the Bride's home to collect her for the wedding, these questions will serve that occasion too.

- ❏ Where did the Bride and Groom first meet?
- ❏ What is the Bride/Groom's shoe size?
- ❏ Where/when was the couple's first kiss?
- ❏ What is the Bride/Groom's favorite drink/restaurant/pizza topping/snack/ice cream flavor/color/animal/sport?
- ❏ What celebrity does the Bride/Groom most want to meet?
- ❏ What musical instrument can the Bride/Groom play?
- ❏ What will their anniversary date be?
- ❏ What is the most important make-up/grooming item to the Bride/Groom?
- ❏ What was the Bride/Groom's first pet/car/job?
- ❏ How many siblings does the Bride/Groom have?
- ❏ What is the Bride/Groom's favorite movie/TV show?
- ❏ Name the friend the Bride/Groom knows the longest?
- ❏ Where/when did the proposal take place?
- ❏ What is the Bride/Groom's favorite kitchen/garden tool?
- ❏ How much did the Groom's tux/Bride's shoes cost?
- ❏ Does the Bride/Groom squeeze toothpaste from the top, bottom, or middle?
- ❏ If they had all the money in the world, where would the Bride/Groom go for a vacation?
- ❏ What is the Bride/Groom's biggest pet peeve?
- ❏ What spice/seasoning can't the Bride/Groom live without?
- ❏ What is the Bride/Groom's funniest idiosyncrasy?
- ❏ What languages does the Bride/Groom speak?
- ❏ What does Bride/Groom keep under his/her bed?
- ❏ Who traveled the farthest for the wedding, from where?

50-50 QUESTIONS

Query the Bride and Groom with the questions below in the Best Friend Vs. The Groom game. Feel free to tailor additional queries to the couple's likes or dislikes.

- ❏ Decaf or sugar-free cola?
- ❏ Motorcycle or convertible?
- ❏ Gardening or reading?
- ❏ Chocolate chip or sugar cookie?
- ❏ Music, loud or low?
- ❏ The side of the bed or the middle?
- ❏ E-mail or phone call?
- ❏ Dogs or cats?
- ❏ Cubed or crushed ice?
- ❏ Driver or passenger?
- ❏ Sneakers or dress shoes?
- ❏ Banana or melon?
- ❏ Monopoly® or Candy Land®?
- ❏ Dishwashing gloves or bare hands?
- ❏ Movie theater or video rental?
- ❏ Spicy or mild?
- ❏ Mountain or beach?
- ❏ Croutons or no croutons?
- ❏ Toilet paper, over or under?
- ❏ Sun or shade?
- ❏ Humming or whistling?

COMPARATIVE QUESTIONS

These questions are suggested for the Shoe-In game.

- ❏ Who drives the fastest?
- ❏ Whose cooking is better?
- ❏ Who controls the TV remote?
- ❏ Who can't wait to get out of their tux or dress the fastest?
- ❏ Who is more spontaneous?
- ❏ Who spends the most time taking a shower?
- ❏ Who's more tired?

- Who takes the longest to order at a restaurant?
- Who gets more e-mails in a day?
- Who has the greenest thumb?
- Who eats more junk food?
- Who wakes up earlier in the morning?
- Who was the first to speak when you two first met?
- Who owns the most clothing?
- Who is the neatest?
- Who will hog all the bed covers at night?
- Who is the cutest?*
  (*Save this question for last, since the Bride and Groom theoretically will answer with their beloved--it ends the game on a sweet note.)

ETIQUETTE GAME QUESTIONS

Additional disaster scenarios for adding players to the Etiquette game...

What do you do if...?
- The flower girl and ring bearer start fighting down the aisle.
- One of the guests has fallen asleep during the ceremony and is snoring loud enough for everyone to hear.
- The Bride's bouquet toss accidentally knocks a guest unconscious.
- The Groom cuts a loud fart during the exchange of vows.
- The pastor/officiant never shows up for the wedding ceremony.
- The caterer refuses to serve the reception until an additional $1,000 is paid to cover a last-minute food substitution.
- One of the guests' children accidentally gives the Groom a black eye an hour before the wedding.
- The band for the reception has left for their next gig because the wedding ran late.
- The maid of honor gets the hiccups during the ceremony.
- An unusually hot day causes all the icing decorations on the wedding cake to melt and slip off the cake.
- You've lost the wedding rings the day of the wedding.
- The wedding limousine never shows up after the ceremony.
- The singer at the reception sings so badly everybody notices.
- The Groom's ex asks if she should tell him she still loves him.

Make a photocopy of this story and wherever the words are in all caps, fill in substitutions given by your players:

I once had a crystal ball that told me the future. It even predicted that BRIDE'S NICKNAME and GROOM'S NICKNAME would tie the knot. This incredible, ADJECTIVE ball thought the ADJECTIVE newlyweds were going to beautiful NAME OF COUNTRY for their honeymoon. It also advised that they stay away from eating any FOOD, but definitely sample their native A DIFFERENT FOOD. This ball says the happy couple are going to be very successful in NAME OF INDUSTRY and CAREER. And success will follow them home, in the future they will have NUMBER children whose names will be SAME NUMBER OF NAMES. They will grow up to be very ADJECTIVE children who love to VERB. A beautiful, ADJECTIVE home with NUMBER rooms awaits them in NAME CITY. And they'll fill their bright COLOR house with gadgets like APPLIANCE and APPLIANCE. And at the ripe old age of NUMBER, they'll retire to COUNTRY and play SPORT and sip ALCOHOLIC DRINK (PLURAL).

BRIDAL/GUEST BINGO CARD

Make copies of this grid for Bridal Bingo and Guest Bingo, enlarge if desired. Fill in the squares per instructions given for each game.

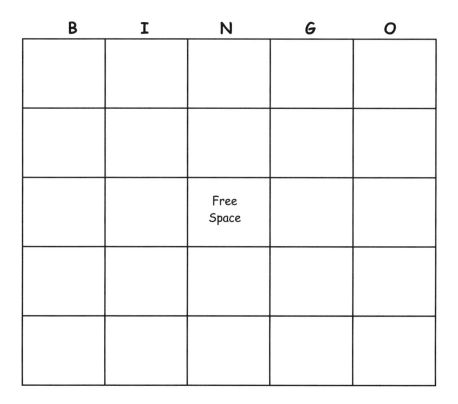

B	I	N	G	O
		Free Space		

To add more to the list, think of popular fictional characters as well as real-life famous couples.

- ❏ Homer & Marge (Simpson)
- ❏ John & Yoko (Lennon)
- ❏ Clark (Kent) & Lois (Lane)
- ❏ Pierre & Marie (Curie)
- ❏ Arnold (Schwarzenegger) & Maria (Shriver)
- ❏ Bonnie & Clyde (Barrow)
- ❏ Rick (Blaine) & Ilsa (Laszlo) (Casablanca)
- ❏ Paul (Newman) & Joanne (Woodward)
- ❏ Lucy & Ricky (Ricardo)
- ❏ Tom (Hanks) & Rita (Wilson)
- ❏ Rocky (Balboa) & Adrian
- ❏ Will (Smith) & Jada (Pinkett)
- ❏ Fox (Mulder) & Dana (Scully)
- ❏ Romeo & Juliet
- ❏ Mike & Carol (Brady)
- ❏ Regis & Joy (Philbin)
- ❏ Michael (J. Fox) & Tracy (Pollan)
- ❏ Howard & Marion (Cunningham)
- ❏ Christopher & Dana (Reeve)
- ❏ Gracie (Allen) & George (Burns)

PENALTIES

Threat of even the mildest public embarrassment usually motivates players to put their all in a game. Penalties may be randomly assigned by having players draw slips of paper from a bowl or insert the paper slip inside a balloon and have guests pop one to discover their punishment.

- ❏ Do a couple of push-ups or hula-hoop for 30 seconds.
- ❏ Put a large marshmallow in their mouth for every wrong answer they give. (This works best when they're answering a series of questions.)
- ❏ Give their beloved a piggyback ride around the room.
- ❏ Wear an article of the opposite sex's underwear (over their clothing, of course).
- ❏ Send the person outside to leave a zucchini on a neighbor's front porch without being detected. Continue to send all penalized players to the same porch.
- ❏ Take a shot. (Use caution when applying alcohol as penalty, space it out to avoid getting players too drunk.)
- ❏ Croon a few lines of a song.
- ❏ Moon the group.

- Affix a feminine pad or tampon on his shirt for each wrong answer given.
- Bawk like a hen, crow like a rooster, moo like a cow, etc.
- Wear an outrageously goofy hat until the next player gets a penalty.
- Speak for a full minute on a randomly drawn topic concerning the Bride or Groom. Topic ideas: dating disasters, cooking or driving abilities, rumors, most embarrassing moment, etc.
- Loser for this game has to volunteer for another game.
- The person receiving the penalty must hold a large brush dipped in paint between their legs and write "I Love You" on a long length of butcher paper held up against the wall at waist level. (Wrap rubber bands around the handle so that the brush is easier to grip.) The hip action is sure to generate laughs.
- Carve a model of a guy's manhood out of a cucumber using only your teeth.
- Charge the Bride or Groom a dollar (distribute the collected money among the bridesmaids and groomsmen).
- Every time the Bride's name is mentioned, the penalized player has to chime in with "to be married on (date of wedding)."
- Dance to 30 seconds of music.
- Make up a story to go with a randomly selected headline from the newspaper.
- Come up with as many words that end with "ing" as possible, and they all have to do with life after a wedding. Some examples: grinning, paying, changing, hugging, adjusting.
- Roll a pair of dice, whatever number comes up dictates how many sentences of marital advice they have to come up with to give the Bride and Groom or the number of kisses to give to someone in the room.
- Take a big bite out of a lemon.
- Tell the penalty taker to come up with a silly dare they'd like to see the Bride or Groom do in the room. Repeat the dare to the audience. Then reveal the surprise: the penalty taker has to perform their own dare.
- Come up with your own... just tailor them to your crowd.

Promising a token prize to the winner is a great way to induce more enthusiastic game play. In games where it's Bride versus Groom only, a generous option is to award all the female observers a prize if the Bride wins or gift all the male guests if the Groom wins. Pick and choose to your taste from the list or let it inspire more gifts. Browse the aisles of stores that sell things for under a buck for additional inexpensive ideas.

- ❑ Candy/chocolate/cookie/mints
- ❑ Candle
- ❑ Picture frame/photo album
- ❑ Potpourri
- ❑ Gift book
- ❑ A box of pantiliners/condoms
- ❑ Plush animal or novelty toy
- ❑ Inexpensive jewelry/make-up/hair accessories
- ❑ Candy jewelry (necklace, ring pop, gum lipstick, etc.)
- ❑ New pair of undies
- ❑ A car antenna ball
- ❑ Bottle of dishwashing liquid/gloves
- ❑ Soap/bubble bath
- ❑ Bottle of lotion
- ❑ An address book or journal
- ❑ Movie tickets
- ❑ One shiny new dollar coin/lottery ticket
- ❑ A bottle of bubbles
- ❑ Corkscrew/bottle of wine
- ❑ Current month's cooking or lifestyle magazine
- ❑ A box of hot cocoa or cappuccino mix
- ❑ Small flowering/evergreen plant
- ❑ A gift certificate for coffee or music downloads
- ❑ Any props used in the game

GAME & ACTIVITY INDEX

MOMS & DAUGHTERS

These warm & fuzzy amusements are suggested for conservative players or a group that spans a broad age range (such as a mother-daughter shower). Mommies and their offspring can work together as a team or try pitting moms versus the daughters.

ROWDY GIRLS

Prim and proper these aren't! Only wild women (and men) allowed to party with this selection...

RECEPTION APPROPRIATE

No guest likes to admit the time-honored reception routine can be time-dragged. Invite guests to play these happy diversions in between dining and dancing, or as an alternative to dancing.

INSTANT PARTY

Maybe you've got no budget, or it's a last minute get together, or you're more of a doer than planner. The games below require zero preparation and minimal supplies (paper & pens). Just add bodies and stir in giggles.

GOING OUT TO PLAY

These games are enhanced in a bar, club, or restaurant setting where a passerby can easily join the fun. Browse the Sit Down Games chapter for good times during the limousine ride in between.

COED CROWD

Showers are less and less estrogen only affairs. Why should the Bride exclude her best guy friends? Try the following for flirty fun or gender-neutral laughs with girls and boys.

GROOM REQUIRED

When a blushing bride just isn't enough! These games or pranks are meant for the engaged/newlyweds to play together. A wonderful way to include the easy-going Groom in quality time with his beloved's friends and/or family.

EVERYBODY'S A WINNER

If non-competition is the name of the game, skip singling out anyone for an award or penalty. Play the following games solely for the joy of playing.